T0087993

TALES FROM THE
ANGELS
DUGOUT

TALES FROM THE
ANGELS
DUGOUT

A COLLECTION OF THE GREATEST
ANGELS STORIES EVER TOLD

STEVE BISHEFF

SPORTS
PUBLISHING

Sports Publishing books may be purchased in bulk at special discounts for sales promotion, corporate gifts, fund-raising, or educational purposes. Special editions can also be created to specifications. For details, contact the Special Sales Department, Sports Publishing, 307 West 36th Street, 11th Floor, New York, NY 10018 or sportspubbooks@skyhorsepublishing.com.

Sports Publishing® is a registered trademark of Skyhorse Publishing, Inc.®, a Delaware corporation.

Visit our website at www.sportspubbooks.com.

10 9 8 7 6 5 4 3 2

Library of Congress Cataloging-in-Publication Data is available on file.

Cover design by Tom Lau
Cover photo: AP Images

ISBN: 978-1-68358-016-4
Ebook ISBN: 978-1-68358-059-1

Printed in the United States of America

For Marsha,
whose love, patience, and understanding have made it
possible for me to work all these years at a job I love.
I couldn't have completed this project without you.
And for our close friends and longtime season ticket
holders, Bernie and Barbara King, who allowed
me to see, through their eyes, the pure joy Angels
fans experienced in 2002 after so many
years of frustration following this team.

CONTENTS

Prologue ix

Chapter 1: **"WIN ONE FOR THE COWBOY"** 1

Chapter 2: **THE OTHER FANTASY SEASON** 9

Chapter 3: **THE WRONG CHEMISTRY** 19

Chapter 4: **THE RIGHT CHEMISTRY** 31

Chapter 5: **OF CURSES, HEXES, AND TRAGEDIES** 41

Chapter 6: **GREAT PLAYERS AND COLORFUL CHARACTERS** 49

Chapter 7: **EVERYMAN'S TEAM** 67
           The Choreographer 69
           The Throwback 74
           The Good Soldier 79
           The Pest 84
           The Series MVP 89
           The Last Angry Closer 94
           The Pure Hitter 99
           The New Ace 104
           The Rockin' First Baseman .109
           The Sudden Hero 114
           The Phenom 119
           The Role Players 124

Chapter 8: **THE SURREAL POSTSEASON** 129

Chapter 9: **THE AMERICAN LEAGUE DIVISION SERIES:**
                    WHAT YANKEE MYSTIQUE? 131

Chapter 10: **THE AMERICAN LEAGUE CHAMPIONSHIP SERIES:**
                    A TWINS KILLING 139

Chapter 11: **THE WORLD SERIES: AND THE FANTASY LIVES** 147

Chapter 12: **MEETING OF THE MINDS** 159

Chapter 13: **THE ALL-TIME ANGELS** 165

PROLOGUE

Fourteen years have whisked by since this book was originally published after the Angels won their first and only world championship. There have been some considerable highs and, yes, more than a few lows during that time frame, but everything about this franchise's past, present, and future changed on a warm spring evening in 2012.

That's when Mike Trout arrived.

They used to call him the "Millville Meteor" back when he was a high school legend in his hometown of Millville, New Jersey, and soon enough Trout could be seen streaking across the major-league landscape, quickly establishing himself in his early 20s as not only the best player on his team, but as the finest all-around player in baseball.

He hits, he runs, he makes spectacular soaring catches in center field, and he lights up scoreboard replay screens everywhere he plays. Dedicated Angels fans may not have been treated to another World Series champion but they have been fortunate enough to watch the most exciting player in the sport on a daily basis.

It is difficult to describe just how brilliant Trout, already the best player in Angels history, has been in such a short span. He has been Rookie of the Year, a two-time Most Valuable Player in the American League, an MVP runner-up in his three other seasons, and the MVP of the All-Star Game in back-to-back years. All of that accomplished before he turned the tender age of twenty-six.

To put it in perspective, consider what Hall of Famers Willie Mays and Mickey Mantle, easily the two most decorated center fielders of their generation, accomplished in their first five years in the game, compared to Trout:

Mays					Mantle					Trout				
Avg.	HR	RBI	SB	OPS	Avg.	HR	RBI	SB	OPS	Avg.	HR	RBI	SB	OPS
.274	20	68	7	.828	.267	13	65	8	.792	.326	30	83	49	.963
.345	41	110	8	.1078	.311	23	87	4	.924	.323	27	97	33	.988
.319	51	127	24	.1059	.295	21	92	8	.895	.287	36	111	16	.939
.296	36	84	40	.926	.300	27	102	5	.933	.299	41	90	11	.991
.333	35	97	38	.1033	.306	37	99	8	.1042	.315	29	100	30	.991

As you can see, Trout's numbers compare favorably to the game's two unquestioned icons, and that's without mentioning the staggering list of other accomplishments he has managed in his first five seasons. For instance, since 1917, only two players in American League history have had seasons where they registered a .950 OPS (on-base percentage plus slugging percentage) and stolen 30 bases—Trout and Ty Cobb. And in baseball's favorite new-stage statistical comparison, WAR (Wins Above Replacement), only two players have led the American League in this category for five consecutive years—Trout and Babe Ruth. Even better, Trout has managed to do it while serving as one of baseball's true role models. No DUIs, no domestic abuse charges, no controversies. He willingly signs as many autographs as possible for kids and regularly makes himself available to the media. He is the new Derek Jeter, only with considerably better offensive numbers.

So yes, Trout is definitely the player of the moment in Orange County, the one shining light that has prevailed even when the dark shadows of a discouraging 74-win season threatened to overtake Angel Stadium in 2016. Trout is the one reason to either come to the ballpark every night or to click on your giant flat screen television to watch the Angels as they attempt to crawl back to respectability.

But already, the worry among some fans is this: If the Angels don't improve, if they aren't able to regain their status as a consistent playoff contender, will they be able to keep Trout after his current lucrative contract runs out following the 2020 season? For all his extraordinary performances, the team has only made it to the postseason once in Trout's brief five-plus-year career. If that disheartening trend continues, will they be able to prevent Trout from leaving to sign an enormous free-agent contract with oh, say, the New York Yankees, or maybe the team he rooted for as a youngster, the Philadelphia Phillies? Or what if their deep-pocketed Southern California neighbors, the Los Angeles Dodgers, decided to throw their top-heavy bankroll at him? It is a scary thought, but there is time for this Angels team to bounce back.

"We are not that far away from being a playoff contender again," says Mike Scioscia, and he should know. Scioscia is the longest-tenured manager in the major leagues, and the man who steered the ship through all the rough waters that led to the 2002 championship. Scioscia is the lone remaining bridge between the Angels' happy past and what he believes can be a bright future.

Certainly, by now, he has seen it all. He has been there for the various playoff runs and disappointments along the way, beginning with Boston burning their chances in the 2004, 2007, and 2008 postseason. The Angels made it all the way to the ALCS in 2005, only to get beat in five games by a Chicago White Sox team that went on to capture the World Series. It isn't like the Angels haven't enjoyed regular season success. They won 94 games in '07, 100 games in '08, 97 in '09, and 98 in 2014, the year Kansas City's future world champions knocked them off in the first round.

They've had their share of great post-2002 players, as well. Bartolo Colon paused amid his long major-league odyssey to win a Cy Young Award in Anaheim. Vladimir Guerrero signed as a free agent and enjoyed a series of exceptional seasons in Orange

County, including a .337, 39-home-run, 126-RBI splash that won him the American League MVP Award in 2004. Others such as Torii Hunter, John Lackey, Chone Figgins, Erick Aybar, and Howie Kendrick helped to keep the team in the thick of things.

Later, of course, owner Arte Moreno stunned the baseball world on a cool December morning in 2011 by announcing he had just signed 32-year-old free agent and future Hall of Famer Albert Pujols to a ten-year, $240 million contract. And if that wasn't enough of a shock, Moreno followed it up by convincing pitcher C. J. Wilson to sign a generous $77 million deal. Two years later, in an apparent attempt to keep up with the free-spending Dodgers in the competitive Southern California market, Moreno made his biggest gamble yet, shelling out $125 million for Josh Hamilton, the ultra-talented slugger with a long history of drug-related problems. That's a $442 million investment that, in the end, failed miserably. Of course, failures can sometimes be deceiving. Pujols, Wilson, and Hamilton certainly didn't deliver anything comparable to their collective price tags on the field. But their presence helped seal a $2 billion—yes, that's billion with a "b"—long-term television contract with Fox Sports West.

While Pujols hasn't been the same great high-average power hitter he was in his prime in St. Louis, he has nonetheless been a consistent home run and RBI producer whose presence in the lineup, directly behind Trout, has certainly helped the Angels become a better offensive team.

Hamilton, on the other hand, proved to be a complete disaster. After failing both on the field and off, struggling with his old addictive habits, he was traded back to Texas by the Angels, who have had to assume much of his monstrous contract even while he has been employed by someone else.

Moreno was a wildly popular owner when he first took over in Anaheim and, in his first public act, immediately lowered beer prices to the delight of thirsty fans everywhere. But he has not been the same since he was roundly criticized for the Hamilton signing. Highly visible in his first few happy seasons in Anaheim, he has become an owner who is rarely seen and hardly ever heard from. He went from a public figure that seemed happy to talk to the press to a seemingly moody man who shunned all interviews. His apparent disdain for the media became evident when he decided to move the Angel Stadium main press box, one of the best in baseball at the time, from behind home plate to far out by the right-field foul pole. He maintained it was to increase revenue by selling the plush new reconfigured seats behind home plate to the public, but most of the media people in the area weren't buying it.

More important to Angels fans, the former free-spending Moreno became tight with his budget. Faced with several holes in their lineup prior to the 2016 season, the owner refused to spend money on any of the high-priced free agents, several of whom would have greatly increased the Angels' chances in the American League West. Instead, the club was left to try and patch holes with journeymen at key positions like left field, second base and in the starting rotation. Moreno isn't losing money with the Angels. Not with all that lucrative TV cash rolling in annually. The question is, did that expensive and very public mistake he made with Hamilton cause the owner to lose his nerve?

The first clues should come from the new man in charge of running the baseball operation. Billy Eppler is the 41-year-old general manager who signed a four-year deal with the club before the 2016 season. He was GM Brian Cashman's top assistant with the Yankees before coming back to Southern California, where he grew up in nearby San Diego. In his first year on the job in Anaheim, it was clear Eppler was greatly limited by budget restraints. It must have been a major culture shock, coming from the big-spending Yankees to the cash-conscious Angels.

As he prepared to begin his second season, however, Eppler seemed confident some of that small-spending philosophy will change. "Arte Moreno and I have had numerous conversations about payroll," Eppler said, "and he wants me to inform him when the right situation comes along. He has indicated he will pay to get the right player at the right time."

The skeptics out there will believe it when it happens. But it should help that some $40 million in salaries to players like Wilson and Jared Weaver are due to come off the books. "That definitely gives us a little more flexibility than in years past," Eppler said.

Of course that's only part of the big job ahead in Anaheim. For several years now the Angels' farm system has been consistently ranked as the worst in baseball. In 2016, most scouting evaluations of the top 100 prospects in the game failed to name even one Angels player. Eppler is hopeful that will change.

"We intend to be aggressive in the draft and aggressive in Latin America," he said.

He is encouraged by the progress of recent draft classes that include promising first baseman Matt Thaiss, good-hitting catcher Taylor Ward, and athletic outfielder Jahmai Jones.

Until some of those kids reach the big leagues, Angels fans will try to be patient. Attendance was down slightly in 2016 but still a robust 3,016,142 for the season. Despite the disappointing performance on the field, baseball in Orange County always will be popular, especially on those summer Southern California nights. And whatever else happens, the fans will still have Trout, at least for a few more years.

They'll have his bat, his arm, his speed, and the smile that always seems to decorate his wholesome face. What makes Trout even more fun to watch is his obvious joy in playing the game. "You're amazed watching him," said Eppler. "Lots of all-star players perform at a high level six out of ten games. The real supreme stars perform like that maybe seven or eight times out of ten. But this guy, he does it nine out of ten games. And he gets so much enjoyment out of playing. You watch, and you're amazed at the character of the man. And it's not phony. It's real."

Trout should be even happier in the final three years of this current contract when he makes a cool $33.25 million a year. The funny part is, by then, it might look like a bargain.

So for the immediate future, there is Trout, a still-effective Pujols, a hopefully rehabilitated pitching ace in Garrett Richards, and maybe a few added pieces that can help make the Angels serious contenders again.

In the meantime, it is fun to dwell on the good times and the great players of the past. Hopefully, this book will allow you to sit back, relax, and enjoy reliving some of the warm, fuzzy memories of that unforgettable championship season of 2002, as well as a team history full of high drama and colorful characters. From the original owner Gene Autry to Arte Moreno, from Jim Fregosi to Tim Salmon, from Nolan Ryan to Jim Abbott, from Reggie Jackson to Mike Trout.

The Angels have been described in various ways through their more than fifty lively years of existence. But one sturdy fact about them always has been evident.

Whatever else you want to call them, they have never been boring.

—STEVE BISHEFF

Chapter 1

"WIN ONE FOR THE COWBOY"

It was always about The Cowboy. Gene Autry bought the team and harbored the dream, and for years Angels players always talked about how they wanted to win for this gentle, unpretentious millionaire who would stroll into their clubhouse wearing his trademark Stetson, sit down and talk baseball with them for hours.

You've heard the term "a players' manager." Well, Autry was a players' owner. He was his sport's equivalent of the Pittsburgh Steelers' late Art Rooney—more beloved pal than stern boss, more of a friend and confidante to the players than the guy who just signed their checks. America's favorite singing cowboy was also baseball's favorite fan, and his love for the game somehow endured, even through all of the Angels' disappointments and frustrations. That's how the slogan "Win One for the Cowboy" originated. Every Angels team, from the beginning, wanted nothing more than to win a World Series for the owner all the players came to revere.

It is an amazing story, especially when you consider that Autry was almost as unlikely a candidate to become a baseball owner as he was to become a movie star. Born in tiny Tioga, Texas, in 1907, he went to work on his first job as a railroad telegrapher at age 18. To help while away the hours, he would keep his guitar with him. "Just so I had something to strum on," he would say. In 1934, he decided to move to Hollywood. Fortunately, he also decided to take his guitar with him.

Three years later, he found himself starring on the big screen as the top Western star at the box office, the country's original "Singing Cowboy." As if he needed further attention, Autry's rendition of "Rudolph, the Red-Nosed Reindeer" became one of the biggest-selling single records in history and an all-time favorite Christmas song for people of all ages. If The Cowboy knew how to sing in front of a microphone and project before the cameras, he also knew how to operate away from them. Autry was nothing if not an astute businessman and soon became a big-time player in the entertainment industry.

The irony, of course, is that baseball wasn't on his mind when, after buying a number of radio stations around the country, he ventured to St. Louis in 1960 to reacquire the radio rights to Dodgers games in Southern California. Walter O'Malley, the Dodgers' own financial wizard, had pulled his team's games off Autry's Golden West Broadcasting–owned KMPC radio station. So The Cowboy was there to try and make peace with the Dodgers.

Instead, he would soon find himself competing with them. After several other parties failed to secure the proposed American League expansion team in Los Angeles, Autry stepped in, obtaining a $1.5 million letter of credit, and soon found himself the owner of a major-league baseball franchise in L.A. The Cowboy had joined one of sports' most exclusive clubs.

"First time in baseball history a franchise has been awarded to a horse," wrote Red Smith, the legendary New York columnist. Some cynics enjoyed poking fun at the story. But many others back home were anything but cynical.

If you were a young baseball fan in Southern California, the news was staggering. The Angels were now a major-league team? It was almost too much to comprehend.

Before the Dodgers moved west in 1958, there was only pro football in Los Angeles. The Rams were the big thing, with their wild, wide-open offenses playing to packed houses in the Coliseum. If you loved baseball, you were left to watch the old Pacific Coast League, which seemed entertaining enough, especially if you enjoyed being close to the action. First, of course, you had to choose. Either you were a fan of the Los Angeles Angels or the Hollywood Stars. It had to be one or the other. It couldn't be both.

Maybe it wasn't as fierce a rivalry as the Brooklyn Dodgers and New York Giants, but in L.A., it had to suffice. And at games played in folksy Wrigley Field and at tiny Gilmore Field, long, warm afternoons munching hot dogs and watching the likes of Steve Bilko and Carlos Bernier, Gene Mauch and Dick Stuart, Chuck Connors and Bill Mazeroski were more than enough to turn you on to America's national pastime.

But then the Dodgers moved to Los Angeles. The PCL was gone and longtime Angels fans were excited and saddened at the same time. That's why the news two years later, that the Angels— this time the big-league Angels—were coming home was such a cause for celebration. I mean, the Dodgers were exciting enough, but these were the Angels—*your* Angels—coming back to play against the Yankees and the Red Sox and the Indians. Life just didn't get any better than that.

It would be nice to say that Autry and the Angels started out in a blaze of glory and galloped their way happily through many championship seasons. But it didn't happen, although a surreal run at the American League pennant in only their second season was almost enough to make everything seem worthwhile, at least for a few more years.

Autry, always the optimist, tried to smile his way through the many disappointments, but sometimes even he grew discouraged. "In the movies, I never lost a fight," he once said. "In baseball, I hardly ever won one."

What he did win was the everlasting admiration of those who played for him.

"From day one, he used to come down and hang around with the players," said Buck Rodgers, one of the original Angels who would later manage the club. "[Jim] Fregosi and me, we were just kids, but we'd all sit around after a game, drink beer for 45 minutes and listen to The Cowboy tell stories. He was very personable, very concerned about our welfare."

"I don't think anyone ever had a bad thing to say about Mr. Autry," said Dean Chance, who won the only Cy Young Award in the franchise's history in 1964. "He was simply a wonderful, nice person. And he really did love baseball. You could tell that just by sitting and talking with him. But he never stuck his nose in. He didn't try to be a pushy owner. The great thing was, he seemed like just one of the guys."

"I think what struck you about him," said Bobby Knoop, the finest defensive second baseman the Angels have had, "is that for someone so successful and wealthy, he was such a kind and humble man. He never criticized us, even when we had bad seasons. He was just a friend. Even though he was our owner and our boss, whenever he was around, he made you feel he was there for us, not that we were supposed to be there for him."

Was there an adjustment period? Sure. It took The Cowboy a while to get everybody's name right. Shortly after he was awarded the franchise, he made it clear that his No. 1 choice for manager was Casey Stengel. When he couldn't land the ex-Yankee Hall of Famer who eventually went to the Mets, he shrugged his shoulders and said, "We couldn't get Casey, so we got this Wrigley guy."

His name wasn't Wrigley, it was Rigney. And Bill Rigney went on to give his new boss perhaps the greatest single managing job in modern history, directing the second-year expansion Angels to first place at the halfway point of the American League season in 1962—when the Yankees had Mickey Mantle and Roger Maris in their prime—and keeping them in contention right until the final weeks of September.

The problems of skyrocketing costs and off-the-field complications came later, after Autry had the good sense to move his team from Wrigley Field and Chavez Ravine to Anaheim, where it could escape from the Dodgers' ominous L.A. shadow and form its own identity.

Once he settled in, he reveled in owning a big-league club. Whether he was hosting a former president, like Dwight Eisenhower, or a future president, like Richard Nixon, in Palm Springs for spring training or just climbing aboard a bicycle and riding to work with his guys in his favorite desert town, The Cowboy seemed to love his new role.

He rode the ups and downs of this franchise as gracefully as he rode Champion, his famous horse. His first wife, Ina, died, but he later remarried. Jackie, a banker who was thirty-four years younger, proved a doting, devoted wife who often chauffeured him to Anaheim for games from their Studio City home. Skeptics often questioned the age difference between the two, but those who knew Autry best said that he was deeply in love.

If all was well with his personal life, the business side of baseball sometimes soured him. He wanted it to stay the way it was, within financial reach of families and children. He worried for the future of a game that was more concerned with building luxury suites than enticing fresh-faced kids to the ballpark.

Autry amazed his friends and employees by handling the Angels' biggest disappointments so well. In 1986, after the Angels lost the ALCS when they were just one strike away from clinching a World Series spot in Game 5, anguish was rampant throughout Anaheim Stadium. Fans cried, announcers were emotionally wrought, and team executives were muttering in disgust.

But The Cowboy said it was OK. He was ready to forgive "the boys," as he liked to call them. He said they would have other chances in the future.

Hope was Autry's lifeline. He never seemed to lose it. As he aged and his body failed, he endured a series of eye surgeries, a hip replacement, and general failing health. But this man who grew to be a legend never seemed to let it get him down.

"I don't know, I've never considered myself a legend or anything like that," he once said. "I've loved everything that I did. I loved radio. I was happy when I was making movies and records. They're all favorites of mine. I tried to pick songs that would be record sellers. Sometimes I'd hit and sometimes I'd miss. I was pretty lucky. I had a lot more hits than misses."

Not in baseball, of course. In baseball, he had more misses than hits. And he admitted his biggest disappointment was "not being in the World Series. We've knocked on the door a few times. But we didn't make it."

The Cowboy could be free with his money, but he could also be frugal. Once, when the owner joined some players on a pre-season ticket caravan to Apple Valley, just outside L.A., they wandered into a hotel that featured Trigger, Roy Rogers's old horse, stuffed and mounted.

Autry was impressed. Someone wondered if he'd consider doing the same thing for his horse, Champion. "I don't know," Autry said. "How much did it cost?"

Informed that the price was $3,000 to $4,000, The Cowboy smiled. "Well," he said, "maybe we should just bury the son of a gun."

One of Autry's happiest nights was when the renovated Edison Field opened in 1998. Wearing that familiar 10-gallon hat as he was driven out onto the infield in a golf cart before the game by his longtime employee and friend John Moynihan, his face beaming, the music playing, the crowd and the players gathering en masse to give him a long, loud, heartwarming ovation, Autry struggled to the microphone, looked up, and said, "I feel like I'm back in the saddle again."

In the Angels' hearts and memories, it will always seem as if he never left, even though he died on October 2, 1998. And that's why there were so many teary eyes and heavy hearts, even in the glow of the team's greatest achievement this past season.

In the giddy, on-field celebration after the victory in Game 7 of the World Series, Autry's wife, Jackie, waved his old white 10-gallon hat into the sky, then gently placed it on the heads of a couple of her favorite players, David Eckstein and Tim Salmon.

"Gene never lost hope, even after 1986," said Jackie. "He always had the hope that if we didn't get them this year, we'd get them next year."

Well, after "next year" finally arrived, it was left for the veteran Salmon, who was lucky enough to be coming up when Autry was still around, to sum it up for everyone after the team had won the American League pennant and clinched its first-ever appearance in the World Series. Salmon said not to grieve that The Cowboy didn't live to see this.

"Oh, he was here," the outfielder said. "He was definitely here. You could feel it. You just know he was looking down at all this and smiling."

He had it right. After all these years, the Angels finally had done it.

They had finally "Won One for the Cowboy."

Chapter 2

THE OTHER FANTASY SEASON

Before 2002, there was 1962. Call It the Angels' *other* fantasy season.

In the second year of their expansion existence, sharing Chavez Ravine, or Dodger Stadium, with their glitzier, more glamorous rivals, the Angels were looked upon more as a novelty—that funny little team that provided something for baseball fans to do when the Dodgers were out of town.

They didn't have a Sandy Koufax or a Don Drysdale or a Maury Wills. What they did have, it turned out, was a wild, crazy, colorful bunch of guys who, in their own way, set the tone for the Angels championship team that would arrive some forty long years later. These 1962 Angels were "scrappy," a term often associated with the 2002 club. They gave their manager an ulcer and drove their general manager crazy with their off-the-field exploits. But they battled you. They hung in when no one thought they could, and if they didn't quite pull it off, they came closer than anyone could have imagined.

This team, in only its second year, with a rag-tag bunch of players other clubs didn't want, was in first place in the American League (there were no separate divisions yet). They were first place in the same league with the New York Yankees, with Mickey Mantle, Roger Maris, Yogi Berra, Whitey Ford, Bill Skowron, Elston Howard, etc. Not only that, these shocking Angels were still in the thick of the race, only four and a half games out of the lead, on Labor Day.

It began with their manager, Bill Rigney, the skinny, bespectacled baseball genius who provided the foundation for this franchise.

"Rig did the greatest one-year job of managing I've ever seen," said Buck Rodgers, the catcher on that 1962 team.

"They were a bunch of ragamuffins, but they played their heart out for him," said Tommy Ferguson, who was the team's traveling secretary.

"I think Rig was the first one to use a double switch," said the late Irv Kaze, who was the team's PR man. "Rig knew exactly how to get the most out of the players. He used Jack Spring [a left-handed reliever who usually would pitch to just one batter] to perfection that year. It seemed like Jack retired every left-handed hitter he faced that season."

Rigney had to be more than a strategist. He had to be a master manipulator and a leader who was patient enough to handle the wildest bunch of characters this franchise has ever had on one team. There was little Albie Pearson, Leon "Daddy Wags" Wagner, Bo Belinsky, Dean Chance, Ryne Duren, and Lee "Mad Dog" Thomas. And then there was Dan Osinski, a powerful relief pitcher who forever etched his name in Angels lore one night when he picked up sportswriter Bud Tucker and dangled him by his heels out the window of a 15th-floor hotel suite. Tucker, who was famous for his one-liners, later said his only fear was that somebody would hand Osinski a drink and the pitcher would drop him reaching for it.

Bo Belinsky wasn't the best player, or even the best pitcher, on the team, but he was undeniably the poster child for this

Left-handed pitcher Bo Belinsky pitched a nine-strikeout, four-walk no-hitter as a rookie for the Los Angeles Angels against the Baltimore Orioles at Dodger Stadium in 1962, the first major-league no-hitter on the West Coast. *AP/WWP*

swashbuckling 1962 crew. For one magical season, Bo was the Joe Namath of baseball. He had a pitch and a beautiful woman for every occasion.

If he had come swaggering onto the scene in the 1980s or 1990s, he would have been the hottest thing going. His handsome face would have been all over *SportsCenter* and many of his late-night exploits would have kept the tabloid TV shows working overtime.

"I tried to room with him for awhile," said Pearson, the diminutive center fielder. "But all I ended up rooming with was his luggage. Oh, man, did he love the ladies. And the ladies loved him. I remember once in Palm Springs, the phone rings and he gives me the receiver to make sure I believe him. On the other end are Mamie Van Doren and Tina Louise [two of Hollywood's leading starlets of the time] and both were saying they wanted to marry Bo. I'm not kidding. Not just one, but both wanted to marry him."

It all came off as a publicity stunt at the beginning. Drafted out of the Orioles' organization, Belinsky arrived at spring training, this street-smart kid from Trenton, New Jersey, and immediately announced that he was all about shooting pool by day and enjoying "broads," as he liked to call them, by night. At a poolside press conference in the desert, Bo immediately captivated members of the Los Angeles media, especially Bud Furillo, who was the beat man for the *Los Angeles Herald-Examiner* at the time.

"When he first showed up, Bo was such great copy," Furillo said. GM Fred Haney offered him a minimum salary of $6,000. Belinsky, who had never pitched in the major leagues and had a 32-35 career record in the minors, scoffed at it. And the writers raced to their typewriters to tell the city about this crazy new left-hander.

Then the season started, and suddenly the Belinsky story didn't sound so crazy. He opened up 4-0 and in his fifth start pitched a no-hitter against Baltimore, the team that had let him go, on May 5. It was the first no-hitter ever at Dodger Stadium, where Koufax and Drysdale worked on a regular basis.

Now the Bo legend really heated up. Walter Winchell, the influential syndicated columnist, discovered Belinsky and was suddenly a regular in the Chavez Ravine press box. Soon, his columns were full of Bo items, with the eclectic pitcher dating this starlet or that starlet. He was with Mamie in this nightclub or with Ann-Margret in that one. It was all Bo, all the time, and nobody loved it more than Belinsky, who bought himself a candy apple red Cadillac with a bonus he received for the no-hitter. He and that car were soon nightly fixtures on Sunset Boulevard.

"The only problem with Bo was that he lacked concentration," Furillo said.

"He couldn't focus on the games. If he could, he would have been something special."

Belinsky's 6-1 record began to show the effects of all that night life. He lost six of his next seven decisions in what would lead to a decline that was almost as swift as his ascent. But that didn't stop him and his pitching buddy Chance from forming one of the sport's strangest alliances—Bo, the pool-hustling slickster from New Jersey, and Dean, the country boy from a farm in Ohio, who proved to be an even better prospect than his new friend.

"For me, 1962 was the greatest year I ever had in my life," Chance said. "We were in the thick of the pennant race; everybody did their little thing. It was unbelievable. But it was even more amazing off the field. I think Bo was the one who had more fun than anybody in baseball.

"I couldn't believe it. Mamie Van Doren said Bo was like a Greek god. She was always around him. And if she wasn't, all these other beautiful women were. Pitching in L.A., I was amazed. One day, on my birthday, actually, they told me somebody special was at the gate. I asked them who it was. They said it was Marilyn Monroe. Turns out it was her birthday, too. That's the way it was for us back then. Sinatra, Danny Kaye, everybody who knew Gene Autry—they were all coming to our games. It was incredible."

The Angels' colorful cast was almost as much fun to watch on the field as it was off the field. There was Pearson, the five-foot-five, 140-pound center fielder who was one of the better leadoff hitters in the game and a perfect foil for all the practical jokers on this rollicking band of misfits.

A year earlier, Ted Kluszewski, the massive first baseman who had made a name for himself by cutting off the sleeves of his uniform because they didn't provide enough room for his huge, muscular arms, was Albie's roommate. They were an instant odd couple. Fortunately, they had a sense of humor about it.

"First thing Klu did," said Pearson, "was tell me not to mess with him. He said if I did, he'd put our two beds together and make me sleep in a drawer."

Then, on off days, Kluszewski and 260-pound first baseman Steve Bilko would escort Pearson to the movies. "They thought it was funny to buy two adult tickets and try to get me in for a kid's admission," Pearson said. "I didn't blame them. I did kind of look like a hot dog between two buns."

The 1962 team was full of overachievers who worked hard and played hard. There was Wagner, an impressive left-handed power hitter who led the team in home runs, with 37, and RBIs, with 107, in that glorious 1962 season. "Daddy Wags" liked a good time and he was known to have an occasional drink or two. Sometimes right up until game time.

"I remember one day in L.A., his hometown, Leon comes up to me and says, 'Tittle Man, I'm not feeling real good today,'" Pearson said. "'Would you take everything you can to my left?' I got a whiff of his breath, and man, it almost knocked me over. You know, I think I led the league in putouts that year."

"Anyway, Wags comes up in the third inning and he just crushes one about 400 feet. It goes out of the park and helps us win the game. I couldn't believe It. Here he was, half-drunk, and he still had enough ability to hit a home run. The guy could just flat-out hit. He had this weird split grip, where his hands were apart on the handle. But he was about six foot one, 205 pounds with a 31-inch waist. He looked like an Adonis. God gave him the gift of a great body. I just wish he would have had the work ethic to go along with it."

Ryne Duren was another who was known to imbibe. He was also one of the most intimidating pitchers in baseball, with thick, Coke-bottle glasses and a fastball that could register upwards of 100 mph on the radar gun.

The problem was keeping him sober enough to pitch well. One night, when Duren was causing a ruckus in a Baltimore hotel, starting pitcher Eli Grba was worried that it would lead to a visit from security. So, the story goes, he emerged from his room in his underwear, walked over to Duren, and flattened him with one punch. Then he picked up the relief pitcher, threw him over his shoulder, and carried him down five floors to his room, where he put him in bed safely, at least for one night.

Ross Newhan, the Hall of Fame baseball writer and Angels historian, in his revised edition of *The Anaheim Angels*, noted that it was "one of the few times starter Grba was credited with a save on behalf of reliever Duren."

"I remember the first time I faced Duren; he was still with the Yankees," said Pearson. "Well, I look over, and I see Yogi [Berra] leaning way over on the outside part of the plate. I asked him what he was doing. Yogi says he has to do that, or Duren can't see his fingers. I'm thinking this guy throws 100 [mph] and he can't see Yogi's fingers? Oh my goodness!"

"When he got to us, Ryne was a real hellraiser. I remember one time they found him laying on the railroad tracks. They had to stop the train to save him. He was loaded, I guess. That was pretty chilling. If he could have stayed sober, there's no telling what he would have accomplished in baseball. But from what I've heard, he's on the wagon now and is a real strong Alcoholics Anonymous guy. I was glad to hear that. Man, I'll tell you what. In his playing days, he could really bring it."

Through it all, through all the partying and the drinking and the womanizing, this team still managed to mesh into a shockingly consistent contender. First baseman "Mad Dog" Thomas, nicknamed for his renowned temper, joined Wagner to hit 26 homers and drive in 104 runs. Rodgers hit .258 and drove in 61 runs to finish second to the Yankees' Tom Tresh in Rookie of the Year balloting. Second baseman Billy Moran hit 17 home runs and had 74 RBIs. And Pearson was a revelation at the top of the batting order.

The pitching, buttressed by a strong bullpen, was led by Ken McBride (who won 10 games in a row at one point), Belinsky, and Chance, the raw-boned right-hander with the unorthodox peek-a-boo delivery. Two years later, in 1964, manager Bill Rigney would call Chance "the best right-handed pitcher I've ever seen." He wasn't quite there yet in 1962, but he finished with 14 victories and a 2.96 ERA. And he dominated the Yankees like no other pitcher of that era.

"I remember one night, I was pitching against Mickey [Mantle]," Chance said. "I had him 0-2, and I threw this cross-seamer that almost hit him. He came up to me the next day in batting practice and he told me when I threw that pitch, he almost wet his pants.

"I don't know what it was about pitching against the Yankees. They had so much power all up and down their lineup, you really had to hump up against those guys. But whatever the reason, I seemed to do well against them."

Pearson said that was an understatement. "When Dean came along, all he had to do was throw his glove on the mound against the Yankees. That would be it. They'd be done," he said. "I can still

Dean Chance won the Cy Young Award in 1964, when he was only 23 years old. Here he is pitching on June 12, 1966. *AP/WWP*

remember Bill Skowron telling me that when Dean was on the mound, all he wanted to do was sit in the dugout."

There was no telling where these wild and crazy guys might have finished in the 1962 race if they hadn't lost two of their best pitchers on successive days in August. Art Fowler, another of their top-notch relievers, was hit on the side of the head during batting practice and was out for the remainder of the season. Then McBride, the ace of the staff while Chance was still maturing, cracked a rib and wound up with only one more decision in the final seven weeks of the year.

Although the Angels returned for the final homestand of the season still within four games of first place, reality and a lack of pitching depth finally caught up to them. They lost six games in a row and 12 of their final 16 in September, finishing 10 games behind when it was all over.

The final slump should not have diminished the season-long achievement. Rigney's managing job was among the finest seen in baseball in that era. And forty years later, it still qualifies among the best. He often joked about the makeup of the team, but he always emphasized the same thing.

"They had character," he said.

They scrapped and hustled and played together, getting every ounce out of their ability—much like another storied Angels team would do in a similar fantasy season forty years later.

Chapter 3

THE WRONG CHEMISTRY

It isn't like the Angels didn't try during their first forty-one years. That was the whole point. They tried almost everything.

It's just that nothing seemed to work. If they had the right manager, they didn't have the right general manager. If they had enough hitting, they didn't have enough pitching. No owner in baseball wanted to win more than Gene Autry. It's just that while The Cowboy's intentions were good, the same couldn't always be said for his baseball decisions.

Where else have they employed seven managers in one six-year run? Where else have they ever had two general managers at the same time? Where else would a manager such as Gene Mauch win two division titles and wind up resigning not long after each one? Where else were two of the owner's longtime favorites as players promptly fired as managers?

Maybe the biggest problem with this franchise is that there was never a plan. There was always an experiment. One regime would try to build up the farm system. The next one would concentrate on signing expensive free agents. Partly because of impatience and partly because it is the nature of the business, Autry never could assemble a combination, or a philosophy, that would work over the long haul.

The Angels tried almost as many general managers as managers, from Fred Haney, the original, to Dick Walsh, Harry Dalton, Buzzie and Bill Bavasi and Mike Port. And who can ever forget that rare combination of Whitey Herzog and Dan O'Brien, who served as general managers at the same time in the 1994, with Richard Brown, a respected lawyer but a non-baseball man, as president?

Of all their general managers, Buzzie Bavasi was probably the most colorful. A longtime successful executive with the Dodgers, he also spent years with the money-strapped, cellar-dwelling San Diego Padres before coming to Orange County to join in on the fun. Autry originally named him vice president and chief financial officer. But soon after he told then-GM Dalton to cut $400,000 from his player-development budget, Dalton left and Bavasi took over as GM.

Buzzie was a baseball old-timer, sort of a charming curmudgeon who loved to play himself against the media and, often, against his own players. He'd tell you one thing one day, then wink and say he was only kidding the next. He had one press box wrestling incident with a writer from the *Orange County Register* and several run-ins with other writers. But that was nothing new. He'd done that in San Diego, too.

What made him different in Anaheim was his penchant for getting under his players' skin. Even though he signed many of the expensive free agents who would come to the Angels in the mid-70s, he never quite adjusted to the modern salaries after enduring holdouts in his Dodgers days with some of the greatest players of that era. So if he thought a player wasn't producing what they were paying him, he'd let him know, often through the newspapers. He and Don Baylor, who won the only MVP trophy ever awarded an Angel, never got along. And although Buzzie did some good things in his years on the job, he'll always be remembered more for allowing Nolan Ryan, the most popular player the Angels ever had, to leave for a lucrative free agent deal in Houston.

Bavasi's quote at the time still ranks among the most infamous in Angels history: "All I have to do is find two pitchers capable of going 8-7 each," he said, referring to Ryan's 16-14 record the previous season. Later, after he left the Angels, Buzzie would admit that letting Ryan go was the biggest mistake he made on the job.

The Angels, of course, were guilty of making many mistakes. They tried a proven, hard-edged man in Dick Williams as a manager and a gentler college coach named Bobby Winkles as another. They even took a reluctant but respected pitching coach in Marcel Lachemann and made him the manager, although even he admitted later that he was never comfortable in the role.

They had former team heroes like Jim Fregosi and Buck Rodgers take their shots and allowed Gene Mauch, one of baseball's most intelligent and controversial managers, to have two different turns at the position. Always intimidated by the Dodgers organization forty miles up the freeway, they hired away the respected Arthur "Red" Patterson as an executive and general goodwill ambassador. But none of it seemed to work.

At one point, in 1994, the Angels went to spring training with 36-year-old Bill Bavasi as general manager, 35-year-old Tim Mead as assistant general manager, and a 23-year-old named Jeff Parker as assistant director of minor-league operations. The joke was that all of them were riding skateboards to work.

Never was the confusion more rampant than in the summer of 1993, when no one was sure who was in charge of this franchise or where it was headed. Autry was 85, and although his second wife, Jackie, tried to say that Gene was still making the bottom-line decisions, everyone knew she was the one basically taking over—or at least trying to take over and institute a new cut-at-all-costs philosophy. The problem was that she didn't want to be the one out front, acting as team spokesperson.

Brown, the new president and CEO, thought that would be his job. But this bright, energized executive wasn't sure, which was understandable, considering that he had about as much baseball experience as the clubhouse boy. How could he be expected to work with Herzog, an industry legend of sorts and an old Autry favorite, acting as quasi-GM not from Anaheim, but from his home 1,500 miles away in Missouri? Then there was O'Brien, who'd been around baseball for thirty-nine years and knew how to work the back rooms. He probably should have been the spokesman, but again, no one knew what was going on.

So who made the baseball decisions and who communicated regularly with the knowledgeable manager and former Angels catcher, Rodgers? Asked specifically about that one day, Buck looked up at a writer, smiled, and said, "Darn if I know."

Even after the Walt Disney Co. took over in 1996, the trend continued. Disney put Tony Tavares, a former head of Spectacor, in charge as team president, and among many in the front office, the fiery era soon became known as "Tony's Reign of Terror."

A strong-willed, intelligent man with a long business background, Tavares was a baseball fan, not a baseball man. And if he was frustrated by the team's lack of direction, he was often confused as to how to solve the problem. Usually, that meant many of those working for him had to take his wrath.

In September of 1996, Tavares fired Lachemann, who was GM Bill Bavasi's choice. It was clear that the new permanent manager, Terry Collins, would likely to be his choice. As it turned out, Collins, a solid baseball guy, was undermined by some of the veteran players on his team a few years later. And when he "resigned," it became apparent that Bavasi would soon follow. Tavares himself would eventually bolt from the organization, but not before leaving a long list of stories for Angels employees to tell.

There might never have been a more interesting press conference than the one in 1996 when Lachemann was fired during the season and Tavares, frustrated like so many other Angels executives in the past, let loose with one of his famous tirades.

"This team has too many players who look like they came from Newport Beach, where their daddies and mommies gave them everything they ever wanted," Tavares said.

"I'm telling you right now, there's no way we go into next season with this kind of chemistry.

"We don't want 'I' guys. We want 'we' guys. And anyone affronted by that statement should be. If it doesn't apply to them, they have nothing to be ashamed about."

Ironically, six years later, the Angels finally developed the kind of team Tavares was talking about. And the man he had hired as general manager, Bill Stoneman, was largely responsible. So if Tavares's methods weren't always appreciated, the vision he had even back then was the right one. It was just a matter of finding the proper way to go achieve it.

What made that so difficult was the Angels' penchant for coming close to, but never quite winning the American League pennant and making it to the World Series. Few other franchises teased and tortured their fans this way, and only the Boston Red Sox and Chicago Cubs have created as much disappointment and frustration through the years.

The three bleakest seasons in Angels memory are 1982, 1986, and 1995. Not because the team was inept, but because the talent was there and the pennant was so close they could almost reach out and snag it like a lazy pop fly. Only when they reached for it, somehow, it was no longer there. Only the pain and misery were left.

This, then, is why there was so much happiness and joy and, yes, relief, when the 2002 team finally won it all.

1982: This was the glamour team with four former MVPs on it—Reggie Jackson, Rod Carew, Fred Lynn, and Don Baylor. With

Mauch cleverly guiding them, the Angels finished with a 93-69 record to win their second division championship (the other was the 1979 team that was beaten in four games in the ALCS by the Baltimore Orioles).

This team went into the ALCS against Milwaukee favored and promptly demonstrated why, winning the first two games of the series at home, 8-3 and 4-2. No team in history had ever come back from an 0-2 deficit to win in a best-of-five series. Of course, no team had ever faced the Angels in that situation.

Reggie Jackson, left, hugs the late Angels owner Gene Autry during ceremonies on January 26, 1982, officially announcing that Jackson signed with Anaheim. *AP/WWP*

Don Sutton, who would pitch for the Angels later in his career, beat them 5-3 in Game 3. Then Mauch, who was never afraid to make a controversial move, made one that was argued about for years. Hoping to prevent the series from going to five games, he decided to start 39-year-old Tommy John on three days' rest, instead of saving him for a potential Game 5. The strategy blew up in his face when John was knocked out of the game and the Brewers won easily, 9-5. Then, in the seventh game, the Angels were leading 3-2 in the seventh inning. Milwaukee loaded the bases with two outs. Closer Luis Sanchez was pitching, but Mauch had lefty Andy Hassler ready in the bullpen. The manager stayed with Sanchez, Cooper singled to drive in two runs, and they were the difference in a crushing 4-3 Angels loss.

"What I remember about that series," said Bobby Grich, the All-Star second baseman on that team, "is that we seemed to go back to Milwaukee flat after winning the first two games."

"I don't know what it was, but we couldn't seem to get any momentum going. We didn't play well. We couldn't get over the hump. In all those final three games, it just seemed like we were always one hit short."

1986: From one hit short to one strike away. By far the most devastating moment in Angels history came in Game 5 of the ALCS with Boston.

It had started so optimistically, with Mauch, who had retired and come back again to manage in Anaheim, sending out Mike Witt, who threw a five-hitter in Game 1 to beat Roger Clemens. Clemens had gone 24-4 that year for the Red Sox and was undefeated against the Angels in three starts.

After losing Game 2, 9-2, amid a not-so-funny comedy of errors, the Angels rebounded to capture Game 3, 5-3, and then came from behind against Clemens to win, 4-3, on Grich's dramatic single in the 11th inning.

That set the Orange County stage for Game 5, a game the Angels led 5-2 in the ninth inning. Then Baylor, now with the Red Sox, homered with a man on to cut the lead to 5-4. With one out in the ninth, Mauch strolled out to make the most controversial of all his managerial moves with this team. He pulled starting pitcher Mike Witt for left-handed reliever Gary Lucas. Before the perplexed fans even knew what had happened, Lucas hit Rich Gedman with his first pitch. Dave Henderson was the next batter, and Mauch called in his closer, Donnie Moore.

When Henderson fell behind Moore, 1–2, the place was bedlam. The fans were shrieking, the police were poised to maintain some kind of order, and the Angels players were poised on the dugout steps.

"I can still remember every moment in that inning," said Shawn Green, the Dodgers' All-Star outfielder who was a teenage Angels fan living in Tustin at the time. "I was standing right by the gate, directly next to the left-field foul pole, and the fans were all crushed against me from behind."

"I was never so scared in my whole life. If it had turned out differently, I really think I might have been trampled by the onrushing fans. The place was going totally crazy."

Unfortunately, things turned out the way they always had for the Angels. On a 2-2 pitch that will live in franchise infamy, Henderson hit a two-run homer on a breaking ball that didn't appear that bad on replay.

In their anguish over that moment, many Angels fans forget that their team tied the score and came close to winning it in the bottom of the ninth, when both Doug DeCinces and Grich failed to deliver a clutch hit.

All they could remember was Moore's fateful pitch, a pitch some said the Angels and the troubled Moore never got over.

"It was the strangest thing when Henderson hit that home run," Grich said. "It was like all these ghosts from the team's past

When manager Gene Mauch retired in 1988, he held the record for managing the longest without a pennant. He came close with the Angels in 1986, but lost to the Red Sox. *AP/WWP*

started coming in. You could almost feel them. I was playing first base that inning, and I saw Henderson's ball all the way. He pounded it. The pitch wasn't that bad, knee-high, but low and away. He had to reach way out and extend his arms completely to get at it."

"As he ran by me, I just remember having my head down, with my hands on my knees, looking at the ground. 'Come on,' I was saying to myself, 'tell me this isn't happening.' It was like all the air was sucked out of the stadium. Like nobody was breathing."

Three years later, after a long battle with depression and alcoholism, Donnie Moore critically wounded his wife, Tonya, and committed suicide in front of his two horrified children.

1995: Longtime Angels watchers should have known on August 3; they should have sensed it when shortstop Gary DiSarcina, the quiet leader who was having an All-Star season, broke his thumb and was ruled out for the season. They should have realized then.

Despite an 11-game August lead—despite some furious attempts by GM Bill Bavasi to acquire some much-needed pitching help—the Angels squandered perhaps their best chance to win another division title.

The Mariners roared from behind to tie and then won the division in a one-game playoff when Randy Johnson beat the dispirited visitors, 9-1, in the Kingdome. It was a great September run by Seattle, but it was an even bigger collapse by the Angels, who couldn't buy a clutch hit through the final week. At one point, they would have gone 26 consecutive scoreless innings if J. T. Snow hadn't hit a meaningless two-out, ninth-inning homer at Oakland.

Nobody knew what to say. Nobody knew how to act. The Angels looked like all their curses and hexes had been too much to overcome. It was left for their poor manager, Marcel Lachemann, to try to explain it to the 87-year-old Autry.

"I saw him a couple of days ago," Lachemann said. "I know he's very frustrated. He's been through all this more than any of us. He's tried just about everything during the course of his thirty-some-odd years as an owner to win."

Sadly, the frustrating 1995 season was as close as Autry would come. He died on October 2, 1998, four years before the Angels finally made it to their first World Series.

Chapter 4

THE RIGHT
CHEMISTRY

After all the failures and frustrations through forty-one painful years, the temptation is to say that the law of averages finally caught up with the Angels in 2002. The planets were properly aligned. The baseball gods looked down at all those struggling Angels employees and decided to smile at them at last.

But there was more to it than that—a lot more. Was some luck involved? Most definitely, particularly in the hiring of a general manager and a manager who were both forced to begin at the bottom of baseball's salary barrel. What happened here, though, was the culmination of hours of hard work from some dedicated people, many of whom were no longer around. Those that brought the core of this team together, like Bill Bavasi, Bobby Fontaine, and Mike Port, weren't there to share in the celebration of that first World Series championship. But they deserved a measurable slice of the credit.

So did many of the long-suffering folks in the front office, the Tim Meads and Kevin Uhlichs, the personnel guys and the PR department and the aides and secretaries, as well as the hard-working trainers and clubhouse personnel like Ned Bergert and

Rick Smith. They were all part of getting to this one magical place in time.

But if there was a real turning point, if you had to pick a time frame when the entire chemistry of the organization suddenly swerved onto the right track, it would have to be the three-week span in September of 1999, when first Bill Stoneman and then Mike Scioscia were hired.

More than ever, in that fall of '99, the Angels seemed to need a proven GM, somebody with the experience and knowhow to develop and evaluate talent—someone who wouldn't allow his loyalties and emotions affect his decisions, as some previous men in this office had. Most of all, they seemed to need someone with the strength and respect to stand up to management. Or, in this case, to Disney's intimidating head sports honcho, Tony Tavares.

Frankly, Bill Stoneman didn't seem like *that* guy. The quiet, almost stoic former big-league pitcher didn't have the track record of a John Hart or the charisma of a Billy Beane. What he did have, though, was a long history of dealing with financial problems as the vice president in charge of baseball operations for the Montreal Expos. For a Disney corporation dominated by the bottom line, Stoneman seemed like the perfect choice.

But to the victory-starved fans of Orange County, he appeared to be just another money-conscious executive who was more concerned with saving dollars than winning games.

In retrospect, Tavares was either a shrewd judge of talent or a guy who just got lucky while searching for someone who would take the position at such a low salary range. For years, through the Autry era and again when Disney took over, the Angels were noted for having the lowest-paid front office in baseball. Some of the salaries were so low that they were embarrassing.

And now that the low-profile Stoneman was aboard, his first mission was an immediate one. He had to find a new manager after the ugly departure of Terry Collins. It wouldn't be an easy

Mike Scioscia, left, shares the American League Championship trophy with general manager Bill Stoneman after the Angels won 13-5 against the Minnesota Twins in Game 5. *AP/WWP*

task, considering that everyone in the sport knew this team had one of the more fractured clubhouses in baseball.

Again, it would have been nice to go after a big-name manager, someone who could come in and gain instant respect just by name and reputation. But the Angels weren't about to do that. Tavares never believed managers should be paid like big-time players. He thought that if you had enough talent on the field, anybody could manage. So Stoneman's search was limited from the outset. He couldn't go after the best man for the job. He had to go for the hungriest candidate out there, someone who would be willing to accept an almost minimum wage for the opportunity to manage in the big leagues. A lot of new GMs would have opted for a safer, more experienced choice. Not Stoneman, who demonstrated in his first important move on the job that he wasn't afraid to gamble.

The Angels are fortunate that Mike Scioscia happened to be the right guy looking for work at the right time. The former catcher, who was best known for his tenacity in blocking home plate, had fallen out of favor with his old organization, the Dodgers, although many in Los Angeles felt that he should have been the manager there. The new owners from Fox apparently felt otherwise.

Setting up interviews that winter at the major-league meetings in nearby Dana Point, Stoneman talked with Scioscia, and several others, at length. Then he called the ex-Dodger back for a second interview.

"He was the only one who ever interviewed me," Scioscia said. "I never talked with [Tony] Tavares. It was just Stoneman."

The new GM was impressed from the outset. "He just seemed to have all the qualities we were looking for in a manager," Stoneman said. "He wanted to emphasize the same things we felt were important. And you could just tell he would command the players' respect. Picking Mike was not a difficult process."

This is how badly Scioscia wanted to manage: He was walking into a situation where the Angels appeared more interested in dumping salaries than anything else. They had lost 92 games the year before and were not bringing back Chuck Finley, their best pitcher. Heading into his first season as a big-league manager, Scioscia's pitching rotation appeared to be an old, surgery-ravaged Tim Belcher, an ailing Ken Hill, and three kids who weren't yet ready: Ramon Ortiz, Jarrod Washburn, and Brian Cooper.

Then there was that clubhouse problem. In 1999, if the Angels led the American League in anything, it was in whining, complaining, and backstabbing. Scioscia's first job was to fix that, beginning in spring training. Then he would have time to worry about starting the season without a true No. 1 starter, a legitimate leadoff hitter, a regular second baseman, and an established catcher. "Other than that, Mike," the Angels told him, "good luck."

Somehow, Scioscia did survive, piecing together 82 victories that first season in an impressive rookie year. Things did not go as well in 2001, especially when the Angels turned in another of their familiar September swoons to finish a disappointing 75–87 and lag some 41 games behind Seattle in the American League West. On paper, at least, prospects for 2002 didn't look much better. But that was before the man who proved the most underrated and understated hero of them all made his first Angels appearance.

You had to look hard to find him on that cool January morning, between all the politicians and the cheerleaders and enough fluttering red confetti to make you think you were at a University of Nebraska rally. This was a PR function to start what the team was calling "Red Dawn," which is a nice way of saying the club was changing its colors to a bright crimson.

Big deal. What seemed bigger was the quiet change in the team front office. Tony Tavares had resigned, and a more subdued former Yankees fan from Long Island, N.Y., had taken over. Paul Pressler said that he was just temporarily in charge, but he added that he was in no hurry to find a full-time replacement for Tavares. "I'm having too much fun right now," Pressler said.

Turns out, the Angels' fun was just beginning. In a startling reversal of form, Pressler unlocked the Disney vaults long enough to sign respected free agent pitcher Aaron Sele to a $24 million, four-year contract. Then he okayed the deal that sent Mo Vaughn to the Mets, not for a couple of cheap minor-league prospects, but for Kevin Appier, another established big-league pitcher. A few months later, he allowed Stoneman to sign free agent Brad Fullmer to fill the team's gaping hole at designated hitter.

Best of all, Pressler nixed the one deal that could have killed Anaheim's season. Stoneman had a trade all but completed that would send Darin Erstad to the White Sox for outfielder Chris Singleton and pitcher Jon Garland. Newspaper reports said that at the last minute an unknown Disney executive called off the deal. The unknown exec was Pressler.

"We've got five solid pitchers now, we've got All-Star players. We think we've set ourselves up for success," Pressler said on that cool January morning. Everyone smiled and placated him, but no one really believed him. Not until nine months later.

What seemed to happen in those months between January and spring training is that several of the Angels players started to take notice. They'd been here long enough to know that this team hardly ever spent money in the off season.

Now they looked around, and the starting rotation appeared set, with Sele and Appier, who had won 58 games between them the previous two years, joining Washburn, Ortiz, and Scott Schoeneweis in what appeared to be the finest starting staff this team had assembled in years.

"We've all said we had good teams before," said Tim Salmon, "but this is the first time I think we really believe it. Always before, we were hoping that somebody would take over this position or make it at that position. But look what management did. In Sele and Appier, they went out and got pitchers coming off good years instead of guys they were hoping still had something left in them. And now with Fullmer, we have a real, full-time DH. You look at all that, and you have to say that management went out and filled the holes we had pretty darn well."

Bill Stoneman said he knew things were going nicely when Garret Anderson suddenly walked into his office one day in the off season.

"You know Garret; he never says anything," Stoneman said. "Well, I look up and he's standing there with a big grin on his face.

I looked at him and said, 'What's that grin about?' He said, 'I think we've got a heckuva ball club. I just wanted you to know the guys think we're really going to have a good year.'"

"That's when I knew," said Stoneman, "that the attitude of our team was going to be good. And I still felt that way, even after our poor start."

Ah, yes, that poor start. It was only the worst start in Angels history, with losses in 14 of the first 20 games. The calendar still said April, and already they were 10½ games behind Seattle in the West.

But Scioscia stayed calm, and so did the players. They broke out of it and started winning regularly, posting not one, but two different eight-game victory streaks. But now it was July, and Troy Percival, their closer, was forced to go onto the disabled list for the second time during the season. Stoneman was sniffing around, trying to find some kind of deal to put together to keep the bullpen from falling apart while their leader was out of action.

Then Percival came to him with some advice. "He told me he'd been watching these guys develop and that we didn't need any more relievers. He said this bullpen was really going to be strong. And he was right."

The Angels' winning ways continued to flow through the summer and, with Percival back, into early September, although the Oakland A's were winning just as much, if not more. Soon it became apparent that Anaheim's best chance was to capture the wild card playoff spot. And with eight games to go, they had an eight-game lead and some in Orange County began to think the playoffs were a cinch.

The "Longtime Angels Fan" knew better. As a loyal follower of this franchise, he was born to suffer. And even in their best season in 16 years, that wasn't about to change.

Suddenly, you could feel this team tighten up. You could see it in the players' faces. You could read it in their body language.

The curses and hexes were circling like vultures again, and that eight-game lead with eight games to play had dwindled to just five with five games to play.

The Longtime Angels Fan had to turn away. He couldn't look any more. He kept seeing the ghost of Donnie Moore, the blurry image of an ashen-faced Gene Mauch, the wobbly choke of a finish in 1995. So when Texas came away with a 4-3 victory over the Angels in Arlington, then Seattle came from behind to beat Oakland, 3-2, the same night, that lead had been shaved to four.

The next game was a televised afternoon event in Texas, and the Longtime Angels Fan knew he shouldn't watch. But he couldn't help himself. He knew it wouldn't be good for his ulcer. But he didn't have a choice.

Happily, the suffering finally ended that same fateful day, when rookie John Lackey pitched a strong game and Garret Anderson, who had predicted as much before the season, hit the home run that basically put the Angels back into the playoffs for the first time since 1986.

Once they had made it official, they began tinkering with their plans for the postseason. Lackey already had secured a position in the rotation, and now young Frankie Rodriguez, who had been so impressive in a couple of short appearances, was penciled into the bullpen picture, as well.

"We knew about Frankie all season," said Stoneman. "We talked a lot about him. We knew he was doing very well and handling Triple A just fine after his promotion. But we worried that if we brought him up too soon, would we being doing a disservice to him and to everyone else on the team that was playing so well? But the more we watched him, the more we decided he deserved a shot. I guess you could say that it all worked out very well."

Tim Mead, the vice president in charge of communications, has been with the organization for twenty-three years. He has been through it all in this front office, watching so much futility, so much frustration, so many of the other attempts to find the right combination fail. He was asked to explain what made everything come together so perfectly in 2002.

"I think a lot of things had to happen," Mead said. "First, people were allowed to focus on their specific job responsibility. That was pivotal. But, you know, this was a culmination of a lot of people's work. Tony Tavares deserves some credit; so do Bill Bavasi, Bobby Fontaine, and Mike Port. All of them had something to do with assembling the core of players and management we had this season."

"Paul Pressler was a big key, too. He was hands-on, but at the same time, he knew how to be hands-off in a very good way. He let the baseball people be autonomous, and that wasn't always the case in the past. Paul not only nixed the Erstad deal, but all the money flow went through him. He was huge. He also approved the change of uniform, and people laugh, but that ended up playing a big role. It changed our environment and atmosphere.

"The biggest thing of all, though, is that for once the focus wasn't on money. It was on winning baseball games. If we didn't win, we were going to lose $15 million. Everyone knew that. Even after we won the World Series, we still lost money. But nobody at Disney ever said anything."

"Maybe everybody just kind of grew up a little bit, both the players and the front office. Mike [Scioscia] and Bill [Stoneman] did great jobs. And the fans really stepped up for us, especially in the postseason. That Game 6 should have an asterisk next to it. The fans were fantastic in that one. Now we think our attendance will improve by 500,000 this season. It seems clear we have achieved a certain level of credibility now in both the organization and the community. And you know what? After all these years, it is a very nice feeling."

Chapter 5

OF CURSES, HEXES, AND TRAGEDIES

It was mid-afternoon, a few hours before the Angels were to open the 1999 season with skyrocketing new hopes and a hulking new first baseman. The once-hesitant owners from Disney had shed their frugal image by shelling out $80 million to sign Mo Vaughn, the Red Sox' much-coveted power hitter, to a six-year contract, and it had created a huge buzz throughout Orange County.

As a columnist for the *Orange County Register,* I was heading out the door for the ballpark, my computer bag slung over my shoulder, when my wife, Marsha, suddenly asked, "So what do you think is going to happen with the Angels?"

Almost as a reflex, I smiled and said, "The way things have always gone for them, I wouldn't be surprised if Mo Vaughn slips down the dugout steps in the first inning and breaks his leg."

In the top half of the first inning of that opening game against Cleveland, before the Angels had even recorded an out, Omar Vizquel lofted a high popup in front of the Indians' dugout. Vaughn, obviously anxious to impress his new teammates and fans, drifted over in front of the dugout, straining to make the catch. Then he missed the first step—and the second step.

He went tumbling onto the hard concrete with a thud that must have been heard all the way back to Boston.

Within seconds, my phone rang in the Edison Field press box. "That," Marsha said, "was the eeriest thing I've ever seen. How could you possibly have known that would happen?"

If the story sounds apocryphal, it really isn't. It actually came off exactly that way. You can ask my wife. And besides, most long-time Angels fans in the ballpark could have predicted as much. Vaughn suffered a badly sprained ankle, not a broken leg, but the injury severely inhibited him for much of the season. And that hardly came as a surprise to a franchise that had suffered so much bad luck that many otherwise highly intelligent, objective people actually had begun to believe they were victims of some kind of curse or hex. They wondered out loud if the ballpark in Anaheim actually *was* built on an ancient Indian burial ground, as some had insisted.

Whatever the cause, evil spirits were rampant. A strong argument could be made that no other franchise in any sport had suffered through so much pain and agony, so many crippling injuries and, yes, overwhelming tragedies. In a courtroom, a lawyer wouldn't have to plead the Angels' case. He would merely have to present the following list:

- In 1962, in the midst of the Angels' miraculous run at the pennant in only their second year of existence, Art Fowler, one of their top relievers, was hit by a line drive during batting practice, losing the sight in his left eye and missing the final six weeks of the season.
- In 1964, Ken McBride, the first true ace of an Angels pitching staff, was involved in a car accident, suffering severe neck and back injuries. McBride, who had won 10 games in a row at one point that season, won only four more games his entire career.

- In 1968, Minnie Rojas, who had matured into a brilliant relief pitcher, was permanently paralyzed in an off-season car accident. His wife and two of his three children were killed.
- In 1972, yet another car accident took the life of Chico Ruiz, a 33-year-old utility infielder.
- In 1973, Bobby Valentine, the flashy ex-Dodger who was considered one of the better prospects in baseball, caught his spikes in the fence at Anaheim Stadium, breaking his leg so severely that he would never be a productive player again.
- In 1974 and 1977, two more car accidents took the lives of top prospects. First, 23-year-old left-handed pitcher Bruce Heinbechner died in a springtime mishap. Then 23-year-old shortstop Mike Miley perished in a preseason crash.
- In 1978, All-Star outfielder Lymon Bostock was driving with his family and friends in Gary, Indiana, when his car stopped at a traffic light and he was suddenly shot and killed.
- In 1982, Rick Burleson, an All-Star-quality shortstop acquired from Boston in a mega-deal, tore the rotator cuff on his throwing shoulder in spring training, basically ending his career.
- In 1985, the 2-year-old son of pitcher John Candelaria died after being in a coma since a swimming pool accident at Candelaria's home on Christmas Day the previous year.
- In 1989, three years after throwing the fateful pitch that Dave Henderson hit for the ninth-inning home run, which turned the ALCS in Boston's favor, Donnie Moore shot his wife, seriously injuring her, and then killed himself.
- In 1992, the Angels team bus, traveling from Yankee Stadium to Baltimore, careened off the New Jersey Turnpike, injuring several members of the club, including manager Buck Rodgers, who was hurt the worst.
- In 1995, the Angels were cruising in the American League West with an 11-game lead when Gary DiSarcina, the leader and

shortstop who was hitting .317 at the time, broke his thumb and was lost for the season. Manager Marcel Lachemann's club went into an immediate nosedive, blew the 11-game lead, and eventually lost the division title to Seattle in a one-game playoff.

- In 1996, Michelle Carew, the 18-year-old daughter of Angels hitting instructor and Hall of Fame player Rod Carew, died after a long battle with leukemia at Children's Hospital of Orange County.
- In 1997, Chuck Finley was standing innocently behind the batting cage in spring training when a flying bat hit him in the face, breaking an orbital bone and forcing the team's best pitcher to begin the season on the disabled list. Later that same year, Finley slipped backing up home plate and injured his left wrist, forcing him back onto the DL.
- In 1999, before Vaughn even slipped down the dugout steps, DiSarcina suffered a broken bone in his arm in another freak spring-training mishap, this time when hitting coach George Hendrick swung his bat as the shortstop was leaving the batting cage. Further injuries that season grounded Gold Glove center fielder Jim Edmonds and dependable right fielder Tim Salmon.

It is an amazing list, and that doesn't include everything. But by now, you get the picture. When you combine all the terrible incidents and freak accidents with the three just-missed postseasons in 1982, '86, and '95, is it any wonder Angels fans had begun to believe in the curse?

"It's strange, very strange," Bobby Grich, the former All-Star second baseman, said in 2000. "When Mo went down in the first inning of the first game, I remember thinking, 'Not again.' I just shook my head and thought, 'When is this thing ever going to end?' This team has had more bad things happen than even the Cubs. I don't know how to explain it, but it's there. Didn't somebody get an exorcist over here, or something? If they didn't, they should."

Of all the Angels' strange incidents, the two that were the most devastating and have lingered the longest are Bostock's murder and Moore's suicide.

A $2.2 million, left-handed-hitting free agent who signed with the Angels in 1978, Bostock had hit .322 with the Twins in 1976, then followed it with an even better year, batting .336 to finish second to teammate Rod Carew in the American League.

On September 23, 1978, near the end of his first season with the Angels, Bostock was killed by a shotgun blast while riding in the back seat of a car driven by his uncle. Two women were also in the car. The news stunned the Angels and the entire baseball community. Although he was having a disappointing season in Anaheim, Bostock was a likeable player with All-Star ability who was considered to have a bright future in the game.

Police in Indiana later arrested Leonard Smith, the estranged husband of one of the two women in the car, and charged him with the crime. Smith was later acquitted by reason of insanity. He was released from Logansport State Hospital and allowed to return to his home in Gary, Indiana, because psychiatrists had ruled he was no longer mentally ill.

If the news about Bostock depressed Angels fans, the Moore incident came as more of a shock. This was a player castigated for throwing one pitch, when it was *his* right arm that had helped carry the team to the playoffs that 1986 season.

Moore was the Ralph Branca of his generation. In Southern California, he was remembered in much the same way as Bill Buckner, who committed his famous error in October of the same year for Boston.

With the Angels one tantalizing strike away from making their first World Series, the 2-2 pitch to Henderson was a forkball, and Moore, himself, later admitted he shouldn't have thrown him anything off-speed. Of course, the fact that catcher Bob Boone might have called for the forkball never has been mentioned. And the fact that in the bottom of the ninth, when the Angels loaded the bases and Doug DeCinces and Grich couldn't get the winning run home, is rarely brought up, either. It all came back to Moore. He was always the one Angels fans held responsible.

"He was fouling off fastballs," Moore said immediately after that emotional game. "I should have stayed with fastballs. I'm a human being and I didn't do the job. But I won't blame it on my sore shoulder."

A year earlier, Moore had been as good a relief pitcher as there was in baseball, racking up 31 saves with a 1.92 ERA. In 1986, he had 21 saves with a 2.97 ERA. It was common knowledge that he was suffering from some soreness in his arm, or shoulder. He never complained, though. He never asked to be taken out of an assignment.

Five months after "The Pitch," Donnie Moore sat in a quiet room in Mesa, Arizona, as the Angels opened up spring training and talked about the repercussions. "I've thought about it a couple of times," he said, "but I haven't let it dominate me or anything. I never had thrown that big of a home run before. And you know what? When I looked back on the tape, it wasn't that bad of a pitch. It was a low and outside off-speed pitch. In retrospect, I just think it was a bad selection. He is a breaking-ball hitter. I should have thrown something hard."

"I don't want to use it as an excuse, but my shoulder never was the same after a couple of early games in the cold at Toronto. I didn't realize until a couple of weeks after the season how bad it really was. After all that cortisone and stuff wore out, the arm really hurt."

"I still can't believe we lost three in a row to those guys. I don't think we lost three in a row the rest of the year. If our guys

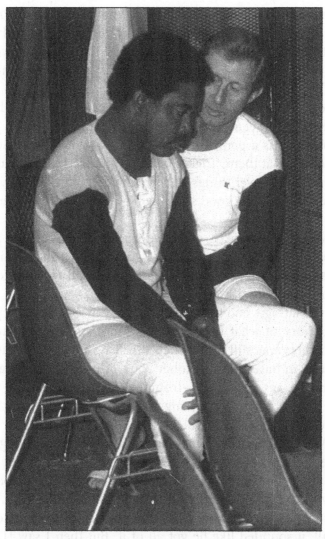

Pitching coach Marcel Lachemann, right, consoles relief pitcher Donnie Moore in the locker room at Fenway Park in Boston. The Angels lost to the Boston Red Sox in the final game of the American League championship series. Moore later committed suicide after struggling with depression and alcoholism. *AP/WWP*

were affected that much [by Game 5] that they wanted to quit, then I don't want to be on their team. I never quit. And I don't expect the guys around me to quit. Believe me, I could have quit many times last summer, the way my arm was bothering me. But I didn't. My pride wouldn't let me."

"Some of the stuff that's happened since has been tough. But you've got to forget about it. I know I have. I made one bad pitch. It didn't cost us a pennant. It cost us a game. We still had two other chances at them. That's one thing you learn in the bullpen. You learn to get over things. I've been up and down before. Anybody can handle the good stuff. It's how you handle the bad that tells a lot about you."

Two years later, in an exclusive part of Anaheim Hills, a tormented Donnie Moore took out a gun and, in front of his two sons, shot and injured his wife, Tanya, then turned the weapon on himself and fired.

It was a tragic end to the saddest story in Angels history, and the memory of what happened to Moore and Bostock and so many others was still there when this team finally won the biggest prize in baseball in October 2002. All the demons—all the rumors of hexes and curses—from the past seemed to hang there, in the cool Orange County night air in Game 7, waiting to be flushed away once and for all.

"Watching the final game that night, it was like reliving 1986 all over again," Grich said. "When the first two Giants got on in the ninth, I was thinking, 'Oh no, not again.' It was almost like you were expecting another disappointment or letdown. We'd seen so many through the years. Even when [Kenny] Lofton hit the ball, it sounded like he got all of it. But then I saw [Darin] Erstad in center field and he was waving his arms like he had it all the way, and then the ball finally came down in his glove. And it was like we had been exorcised. Like all the ghosts were gone. And the air was finally clear."

Chapter 6

GREAT PLAYERS AND COLORFUL CHARACTERS

If the Angels had to wait forty-one years to make it to their first World Series, they didn't have to wait nearly as long to produce a steady succession of great players and colorful characters.

Owner Gene Autry was in the entertainment business, and although he didn't always have the knack for producing a consistent winner, he did have an eye for knowing what would work at the box office. At least in his early years, he wasn't afraid to spend his money, either. So he shelled out whatever was necessary, especially once players gained their freedom and began making themselves available on the free agent market.

When you combine that with the turmoil and, yes, frustration always attached to this team, the one thing you can say about the Angels is that they were never dull. From those first couple of overachieving expansion seasons under Bill Rigney to the surprising champions of 2002, the Angels have been blessed with people who were as charismatic as they were gifted and often as

Nolan Ryan fires the pitch to Brewers' Mike Hegan that secures his 300th strikeout of the season on August 31, 1974. Nolan threw three consecutive seasons of 300 strikeouts. *AP/WWP*

controversial as they were effective. These are just some of the more prominent players and/or characters not chronicled at length elsewhere in this book.

NOLAN RYAN

His fastball is what you remember most. The fastball that passed like a blur through Anaheim—through the record books and through the sacred historical sanctum of our favorite summer game. The fastball that has no equal, the fastball that retained its speed, its movement, and its rare intimidating powers across an extraordinary number of seasons—the greatest, most enduring fastball of them all.

Nolan Ryan's fastball—it made him the first truly great player and easily the most exciting athlete in Angels history. Even today, the memory of it marks him as the most popular player the franchise has produced. He pitched four no-hitters as an Angel, recorded 138 victories and 2,416 strikeouts. But numbers alone don't really tell the story.

"He was the only guy who put fear in me," said Reggie Jackson, back when he was still playing. "Not because he could get me out, but because he could kill me . . . You don't face Ryan without your best. He is the only guy I go against that makes me go to bed before midnight."

"Nolan threw it down the strike zone harder than any human being I ever saw," said Jeff Torborg, who used to catch him. "In 1973 against Boston, Nolan threw a pitch a little up and over my left shoulder. I reached for it, and Nolan's pitch tore a hole in the webbing of my glove and hit the backstop at Fenway Park."

They called him "The Express," and every time Ryan pitched, especially in Anaheim, it was an occasion. You never knew when he might set a strikeout record or rack up another no-hitter.

That is why the Angels' failure to keep him from leaving as a free agent in 1979 still ranks as the most criticized move in their forty-two years. It was caused, some felt, by a rift between the team's executive vice president, Buzzie Bavasi, and Dick Moss, Ryan's agent.

"I thought Ryan simply was asking for too much money," Bavasi said later.

"I think the bottom line was Buzzie wasn't prepared to pay me what we felt like the market was," Ryan said. Whatever happened, even Bavasi came to realize it was a terrible mistake.

"No doubt about it," Buzzie said in 1992. "Gene Autry never interfered with my decisions regarding player personnel, but in retrospect, I wish that was one time he had disagreed with me."

Longtime Angels fans never forgave Buzzie. Even after all these years, many are still bitter about that decision. And when you look at Ryan's record after leaving Anaheim, you can't blame them.

NOLAN RYAN'S NO-HITTERS WITH THE ANGELS

May 15, 1973					
ANGELS	200 001 000	3	11	0
KANSAS CITY	000 000 000	0	0	0
Ryan (W, 5-3) and Torborg; Dal Canton (L, 2-2), Garber (6), and Taylor, Kirkpatrick. (Ryan's strikeout total: 12)					

July 15, 1973					
ANGELS	001 000 050	6	9	0
DETROIT	000 000 000	0	0	0
Ryan (W, 11-11) and Kusnyer; J. Perry (L, 9-9), Scherman (8), Miller (8), Farmer (8), and Sims. (Ryan's strikeout total: 17)					

Sept. 28, 1974				
MINNESOTA	000 000 000	0	0	2
ANGELS	002 200 00x	4	7	0
Decker (L, 16-14), Butler (3), and Borgmann; Ryan (W, 22-16), and Egan. (Ryan's strikeout total: 15)				

June 1, 1975				
BALTIMORE	000 000 000	0	0	0
ANGELS	001 000 00x	1	9	1
Grimsley (L, 1-7), Garland (4), and Hendricks; Ryan (W, 9-3), and Rodriguez. (Ryan's strikeout total: 9)				

JIM FREGOSI

He was the standard bearer, the first real thoroughbred the Angels produced. He came up at age 20 in June of 1962 and immediately electrified the entire organization, from the owner on down. It was difficult to know which one treated Jim Fregosi more like a son, Gene Autry or manager Bill Rigney.

"He was really something when he first came up," said Bud Furillo, who was one of the beat writers that year. "He had all the tools. He could hit for average, he could hit the long ball, he could throw. And he could go from first to third base in a heartbeat."

"He was the benchmark for our organization," said Bobby Knoop, the second baseman who was Fregosi's closest friend on the team. "He had what some people call an arrogance about him. But that wasn't true when you played alongside him. He was a leader, no doubt. Even at a very young age, he was the guy. Nobody had to say it, either. We all knew. He was the one everybody looked at to get us over the hump, to give us a kick in the ass when we needed it."

Fregosi was the team's first real All-Star-quality position player. Statistically, his best year was probably in 1970, when he hit 22 home runs, had 82 RBIs, and scored 95 runs. But like most shortstops, his intangibles were more important than his numbers. Even when he was traded, to the Mets in 1971, it was important. The player he was dealt for was Nolan Ryan.

Fregosi returned to manage the Angels, taking over during the 1978 season. Fittingly, he directed them to their first divisional title in 1979, displaying the same fire and competitiveness he had as a player. He put them on the map and then put them in their first playoff.

As leaders go, the franchise has never had anyone quite like Jim Fregosi.

DEAN CHANCE

You tell the kids today about him, and they don't believe you. "What was his name again?" they ask.

"Chance," you tell them. "Dean Chance." And no one in the frachise's history, not even the esteemed Mr. Ryan, ever had a better single season throwing the baseball than this tall, raw-boned right-hander from the Ohio farmlands.

Consider these 1964 numbers for a moment: 20 victories, a 1.65 ERA, 15 complete games, 11 shutouts, 207 strikeouts, and 278 innings pitched. Against the Mickey Mantle-Roger Maris Yankees during that incredible summer, he was 4-0 with a jaw-dropping 0.18 ERA. He worked in the shadow of Sandy Koufax and Don Drysdale in Dodger Stadium that season and outpitched both of them.

"I was a Cleveland fan as a kid," Chance said recently, "and I always had this kind of hatred for the Yankees. I loved beating them. And I loved pitching against them because there was always a big crowd and there was always this electricity in the air. It felt like a big boxing match, or something."

"The year he had in '64 was unbelievable," said center fielder Albie Pearson. "Personally, I can't recall anyone taking over our league the way he did that season. Maybe Gibson or Koufax pitched that well, but I'm not sure they did. The Yankees would get one look at Dean, and they would go run and hide."

Chance threw a fastball in the mid-90s and fired a wide assortment of sharp breaking stuff from a deceiving, peek-a-boo delivery that left batters frozen at the plate. There is no telling how great he might have been if he hadn't chosen Bo Belinsky as a role model early in his career. They were great friends, but Dean learned how to party almost as hard as Bo, and it definitely affected his work on the mound in his final years with the club.

"Hey, I had a great time," Chance said, reflecting on the 1960s. "It's still fun to talk about those years. We had a great bunch of guys with the Angels."

BOBBY KNOOP

Close your eyes, and you can still see him ranging halfway into right field to swallow up a ground ball and throw the batter out at first. Or imagine him moving smoothly across second base to make a flawless pivot and complete the double play.

Bobby Knoop was all about the leather. His glove was permanently golden. He remains the finest defensive second baseman in franchise history and one of the best in baseball during his era. Knoop and Jim Fregosi were magical around the bag, forming the finest double play combination in the American League.

"I watched Bobby make plays on his head, literally," said Pearson. "The guy could flat play infield. He and Fregosi had a very strong tie on and off the field. They were buds and they went everywhere together. On the field, it seemed to pay off. They had like a sixth sense with one another. I don't care how long I've watched baseball. They were the best double-play combination I've seen anywhere."

Knoop was never a superior hitter, but he had some decent seasons at the plate, especially for a second baseman. He hit .269 in 1965 and 17 home runs in 1966.

"When I look back on those years," said Knoop, who was also a longtime Angels coach, "the thing I remember about those teams is that we all liked one another. It seems to me we did more things together than the players do today. We liked being around each other. There wasn't so much of that side stuff going on. We had fun. That was the best part about it."

THE FOUR MVPs

The Angels were never more exciting, never a bigger gate attraction than when Gene Autry took out his lasso and wrapped it around four of the biggest free agents in the game—Rod Carew, Reggie Jackson, Don Baylor, and Fred Lynn.

When they were all playing together, in the early 1980s, it was like Yankee Stadium West. Writers came from across the country to cover them. Even batting practice became a major event. And you never knew, from one day to the next, when somebody would pop off to the media. George Steinbrenner would have loved it.

Baylor was the only one to win his MVP during his time with the Angels. It came after a monstrous 1979 season, when he hit 36 home runs with 139 RBIs and scored 120 runs. But he was also the one who created the most controversy with then executive vice president Buzzie Bavasi. Carew was the quietest of the group, if not the easiest to approach. But a steady succession of .320-type seasons at the plate made him popular with the fans, especially when he delivered his 3,000th career hit in 1985. Lynn had some big moments with the Angels, such as his 1982 League Championship Series against Milwaukee. But he also had some nagging injuries. Some said too many nagging injuries.

Overall, he never lived up to the potential he had flashed with the Red Sox.

As for Reggie . . . well, he was simply Reggie. Whether he was unloading long, breathtaking home runs or striking out in equally splashy fashion, he was impossible not to watch. "Any place you go, any time he comes to home plate, people get excited," said John McNamara, his manager for a while. "They might walk out to go to the bathroom or to go get a soda. But I don't think anybody walks out when he comes up to hit."

The media loved him. Whenever you wanted a story or a column, Reggie was always there, waiting, although his moods could vary. Say this for him, though, even in the twilight of his career: he always hustled. He ran out every ground ball. He played hard, right to the very end. And he, too, enjoyed a historic moment, launching his 500th career home run in Anaheim.

BRIAN DOWNING

It always seemed strangely ironic that Fred Lynn and Brian Downing would play next to each other in the Angels outfield. They were such complete opposites.

Lynn didn't run as much as glide. He didn't attack a pitch. He stroked it. He was the picture-book ballplayer—smooth, talented, and enigmatic. He might have had more pure talent than any player in franchise history. He just rarely played up to it in Anaheim.

Downing was more the self-made player, a man with limited natural ability who worked and sweated his way into the big leagues. Everything that came easy to Lynn came hard for Downing. If Fred was the executive in his three-piece suit, Brian was the guy out in the street, with his sleeves rolled up, wielding a pickaxe. Lynn was always a center fielder. Downing was a catcher who learned how to play the outfield.

Yet, in the end, it was Downing who had the longer, more distinguished career in Orange County. It was Downing who, until Tim Salmon came along, topped the team in career home runs and RBIs and extra-base hits.

For the Angels, Brian Downing was the ultimate workingman's ballplayer.

ALEX JOHNSON

Ask him to hit, he could hit. Ask him to run, he could run. Ask him to throw, he could throw. Just don't ask him to smile. Alex Johnson never smiled.

He is the only batting champion in the club's history. He was also the only player who was so angry and bitter that he practically tore his team apart. Both his manager, Lefty Phillips, and his general manager, Dick Walsh, eventually were fired as a result of dealing with this man, who reputedly kept a gun in his locker.

"Alex was the meanest, angriest player I've ever been around in the game," said Dick Miller, who covered the Angels back then for the *Los Angeles Herald-Examiner*. "Everybody was afraid of him." Miller should know. Johnson once poured coffee grounds into his typewriter (you all remember typewriters, don't you?).

Acquired from Cincinnati in a 1969 trade, Johnson hit .329 in 1970, edging out Boston's Carl Yastrzemski for the batting title and becoming the first Angel to gather 200-plus hits. But while his hitting ability was unquestioned, he often dogged it on the base paths and generally failed to hustle much of the time. The Angels suspended him once, and teammate Chico Ruiz reportedly pulled his own gun on him in what had to be the scariest clubhouse this team has ever featured.

Johnson's turbulent stay with the club didn't last long. His sour temperament negated his unquestioned talent and he was traded to Cleveland a year after he won the batting title.

CLYDE WRIGHT

He was Gomer Pyle in doubleknits. A lanky left-handed pitcher out of Jefferson City, Tennessee, by way of Carson Newman College, Clyde Wright looked and sounded exactly like the TV character Jim Nabors made famous back then.

Only Clyde could pitch better. He won 22 games for the Angels in 1970 and threw a no-hitter against the Oakland A's, the first one the Angels had since Bo Belinsky shocked everyone in 1962. Wright would go on to have an excellent career with the club, winning 87 games to still rank sixth on their all-time chart.

A smiling, personable man with a terrific, down-home sense of humor, Wright is one of the few ex-Angels to make his home in Orange County. He still works for the club, making public appearances and speeches, often pausing to act like a proud father. Jaret Wright, his son, has forged his own career as a major-league pitcher.

WALLY JOYNER

"Wally World" was a wondrous place to be back in 1986 and '87.

Wally Joyner made such a spectacular entrance at first base for the Angels that people almost forgot the man he replaced was Rod Carew. A smooth defensive player with a textbook left-handed swing, Joyner hit 56 home runs and drove in 217 runs in his first two incendiary years in Orange County, a start that inspired then *Orange County Register* baseball writer Peter Schmuck to rename Anaheim Stadium "Wally World."

Unfortunately, those first two years set the expectation level rather high, and although Joyner proved to be a steady, productive player the next four seasons, he averaged more like 15 home runs and 85 RBIs, which was hardly bad. It just wasn't up to the standard he had set in the first two seasons.

One of the more popular Angels of his era, Joyner eventually left to sign a multi-year free agent contract with Kansas City. For years after, though, you could always spot fans in Anaheim wearing "Wally World" shirts or Joyner jerseys.

JIM ABBOTT

The young man who was born without a right hand didn't realize it, but his mere presence on a big-league mound touched some fundamental emotion in all of us. Watching him out there overcoming his disability to throw baseballs at the best hitters in the world made it impossible not to root for him.

Jim Abbott stirred you. He inspired you. He humbled you.

His first professional appearance in a 1989 spring training "B" game in Yuma, Arizona, drew national media coverage. The No. 1 draft pick from the University of Michigan worked three innings, striking out the first two batters, allowing no runs, only two ground-ball hits, and finishing with four strikeouts. As reporters and cameramen surrounded him afterwards, Abbott sat on a bench outside the locker room and said softly to the writer next to him: "This is ridiculous."

He couldn't understand the attention, but he always handled it with remarkable poise. The word mature doesn't begin to explain Jim Abbott. He was like a 50-year-old in a 21-year-old body. And it was because of his maturity and composure that the Angels rushed him to the big leagues, probably before he was ready. His fastball and slider were big-league pitches, but his curveball was flat and needed more work. Even he admitted that.

Manager Doug Rader loved everything about him and club officials knew he'd be an instant gate attraction. But in retrospect, you can't help wonder what he might have been if they had allowed him to have the full year of triple-A experience he never enjoyed. It wasn't like his career was a bust or anything.

Jim Abbott delivers a pitch against the Red Sox on his way to a four-hit shutout in Boston on August 31, 1989. The left-handed pitcher, born without a right hand, was given a standing ovation by fans at Fenway Park after the win. *AP/WWP*

He won 18 games with a 2.89 ERA in 1991 for the Angels and later pitched a no-hitter as a member of the New York Yankees.

It was just that the superstardom many had predicted for him never transpired.

Not that any of that mattered in the glow of what this courageous Olympic gold medal winner represented to millions of disabled people around the world. Once asked whether he was afraid of stepping out there to pitch against the finest hitters in the world with only one hand, Abbott calmly looked up and said: "I had to stop being afraid a long time ago."

If there was one lasting snapshot—one game that captured everything you needed to know about Abbott—it came early in his rookie year of 1989 when he out-pitched Boston's great Roger Clemens and registered the first shutout of his career against the Red Sox. You had to be there, to be one of the lucky 31,230 in attendance, to appreciate the strong, yet tender emotions that slowly evolved through those final innings. To see Abbott, bathing in the warmth of the crowd's spontaneous standing ovation, trying his best to make decent warmup pitches in the top of the ninth, forcing himself to concentrate on the task at hand, was almost as much fun as watching him retire the final hitter on a meek ground ball to third.

Long after he was finished that night, Abbott stood in the dark outside the entrance to Anaheim Stadium, engulfed by a huge circle of adoring fans, struggling to sign the balls and pennants and baseball cards they were shoving in his face. Chuck Finley, another of the Angels' bright young pitching stars of that season, happened to walk by. Normally, he, too, was hounded for autographs after games. This time, he went virtually unnoticed. Finley looked over at the crowd surrounding Abbott and smiled. He understood.

Everyone understood. The evening, and really that season, belonged to James Anthony Abbott—a true American hero.

JIMMIE REESE

The most beloved Angel of them all wasn't even a player. He was a coach.

In his twenty-three years hitting fungoes and soothing egos, Jimmie Reese, who joined the club when he was 70, proved to be everybody's favorite. He was a kind, gentle man with a smile that could light up a clubhouse. A baseball lifer, Reese once roomed with Babe Ruth, although he joked he never saw him much in the room. Reese played a couple of years in the majors, played twelve years in the old Pacific Coast League, and was honored as the all-time second baseman in that league.

But once he joined the Angels in 1972, Reese was known more for his wonderful manner and his knack for making friends with the players. Nolan Ryan thought so much of him that he named his second son Nolan Reese Ryan. The two were inseparable when "The Express" pitched for the Angels. And when Ryan left, Reese was inconsolable.

"It broke me up; it broke my heart," Reese said. "I didn't think they could do it. I didn't think there was a chance in the world the Angels would let him get away. That anyone anywhere would ever let him get away."

An outsider can't really explain Reese's impact on the Angels through the years. It takes a player who was there.

"To me, he was the consummate patriarch of baseball," said Bobby Grich, the former second baseman. "If ever a person could connect you to baseball's past, it was him. He told stories about Babe Ruth all the time. But the big thing about him was the gleam in his eye when he watched a baseball game. He carried a true love for the sport."

"When you'd do something good in a game, you'd come back to the dugout and after a couple of minutes, Jimmie would get up slowly and walk over to you with those little steps of his. Then he'd put a hand on your knee, look you right In the eye and say, 'Atta boy, Bobby.' It felt like the icing on the cake."

Reese and Grich are among six Angels to have their uniforms retired. The others are Gene Autry, Jim Fregosi, Rod Carew, and, of course, Nolan Ryan.

Jimmie Reese died on July 13, 1994. He was 92 years old.

THE RALLY MONKEY

It was a slice of monkey business that fit beautifully into everything the Angels accomplished in their giddy 2002 season—especially in the postseason.

The Rally Monkey became everybody's favorite visual during the playoffs and World Series, especially when the creative folks at Disney got hold of it and interspersed it into clips of famous movies. Even the opposing players watching from the outfield were laughing.

The thing is, The Monkey worked, too. It popped up on the screen six times during postseason home games at Edison Field, and the Angels clawed back to win five of the six. "I don't knock The Rally Monkey any more," said pitcher Jarrod Washburn, who did criticize it the year before, saying team officials should be more concerned with spending money on players than marketing. "I think he's become a big factor for us. I'm all for him now."

The Rally Monkey was born under innocent enough circumstances. It was a June 6 game in 2000 against the Giants, and the Angels were down by six runs in the sixth inning. A couple of staffers who work in the JumboTron effects department just happened to have a clip of a monkey jumping up and down. They stumbled upon the idea of putting "Rally Monkey" over it and showing it on the JumboTron. As soon as they did, the Angels started to rally. In the ninth, still ahead by two runs, the Giants brought in Robb Nenn, their closer, who hadn't blown a save all season. Up popped The Rally Monkey on the screen, and the Angels promptly rallied for three more runs to win the game.

The Rally Monkey hangs around the neck of a fan outside Edison Field, waiting for his cue to appear and rally the team and the fans. *AP/WWP*

"We consider The Rally Monkey a role player," said one Angels official, tongue planted firmly in cheek. "Our rule is that he can't appear before the sixth inning and he can only show up when the Angels are tied or behind."

Soon enough in October, Angels fans were showing up with Rally Monkey dolls around their necks or hanging from sticks or ropes. The Monkey was everywhere.

Chapter 7

EVERYMAN'S TEAM

Unlike most of the other Angels teams in the previous forty-one years, the 2002 group had no great, single, marquee player—no Nolan or Reggie or Dean. It featured none of the zaniness of some of the other clubs, either—no Belinsky or "Daddy Wags" or Alex Johnson. This was a different kind of team.

This was Everyman's Team. Instead of one overwhelming talent, like Barry Bonds of the Giants, the new world champions had a bunch of very good players who selflessly pooled their talents, proving that the sum can, indeed, be greater than any of its individual parts.

These were not the Lakers with Shaquille O'Neal, Kobe Bryant, and their "supporting cast." This was a bunch of grinding, hustling, blue-collar types. And what made them so spellbinding to the rest of the country was how well they meshed as a unit. Little League coaches across America later wrote in saying it was like watching a manual of "How to Play Baseball." They bunted, they moved runners up, they took the extra base, they were selective at the plate. They did all the little things baseball purists had been preaching about for years.

It was interesting, for those in Southern California, to compare the Angels' post–World Series rally of 100,000 fans in the Edison Field parking lot to the Lakers' massive post-championship parties in downtown L.A. At the Lakers functions, it seemed as if 90 percent of the fans were wearing either a Shaq or Kobe shirt. At the Angels party, there was much more equal representation.

You could see fans wearing Erstad, Eckstein, Anderson, or Salmon on their backs, as well as others with Glaus, Spiezio, Percival, and Washburn. K-Rod, better known as Frankie Rodriguez, had his representatives, as did those proudly wearing Kennedy shirts.

They were heroes, not because of what one of them had achieved, but because of what they had achieved together. The word "TEAM" never seemed more appropriate than when this bunch was on the field in October.

In the following pages, we will profile the key members of this group that so strikingly resembled a true Everyman's Team.

The Choreographer

The manager did more than stand in the dugout, pushing the right buttons and making all the right moves. He molded and shaped this team, working hard through the quiet months of winter to reach the one crucial decision that turned everything around.

It wasn't a change in personnel Mike Scioscia made. It was a change in philosophy.

"I spent a lot of time over the winter thinking about it and talking about it with [coaches] Mickey [Hatcher] and Joe [Maddon]," Scioscia said. "We analyzed what we needed and we knew we were a terrible situational hitting team in 2001. We had to change that. We weren't an overwhelming power-hitting team, so we knew we had to sell these guys on keeping people in motion and moving runners along and making every at-bat a good one. We planted the seed and these guys picked it up and ran with it. In spring training, they were getting on each other if they weren't executing in the situations they needed. When you look back, you realize we made an incredible turnaround that way."

Ask the teams who played them in October. Opponents were flabbergasted at the way the Angels kept raining line drives against them, stretching out every inning, draining their bullpens, scoring runs in torrents.

Scioscia's choreography seemed to meld beautifully with the styles of the Darin Erstads and David Ecksteins and Garret Andersons. It was a perfect marriage, and the honeymoon lasted through seven wondrous games of the World Series and beyond.

"I only hope I don't get spoiled by these guys," Scioscia said.

Fat chance. This is a manager who won't allow himself to get complacent, a leader who doesn't panic, no matter how dire the

Manager Mike Scioscia proudly smiles as he holds the World Series championship trophy. *AP/WWP*

situation looks. He proved that early in the 2002 season when the Angels staggered to a 6-14 start, fell 10 games out of first place in April.

"The impressive thing is that he didn't lose his cool," outfielder Tim Salmon said. "A lot of other guys would have, but he didn't. I think he understands it was mostly a mental deal."

If that was a litmus test for managerial patience, Scioscia came out flashing all the right colors. "What he did was really important," said Maddon, his bench coach. "He knew the early suspensions were killing us. Percival was hurt; Fish and Ersty didn't get off well. But he said, 'OK, it didn't work early. Let's stick with it.' That was huge. He didn't blow up the plan."

Scioscia isn't a screamer. He is a communicator—maybe the ultimate communicator, especially for pitchers. "I think that's the biggest thing about him," said Jarrod Washburn, his ace. "The way he and Buddy [Black, the pitching coach] communicate with us is really impressive. You always know what to expect from the other team when you walk out to the mound. The man caught a lot of years behind the plate in the big leagues, and he caught a lot of great pitchers, too. In my short career, he's the best manager I've ever played for."

This is a guy who came up through the old Dodgers organization, a tough Italian catcher from Upper Darby, Pennsylvania, playing for a loud Italian manager from nearby Norristown, and the temptation was to immediately label him a Tommy Lasorda clone.

Turns out, Scioscia is anything but. Oh, he still pays homage to the man who managed him throughout his major-league career. He is quick to mention he learned plenty of baseball from him. But in style and personality, Scioscia is nothing like Tommy.

Imagine Lasorda in the manager's chair Scioscia occupied early in the season, when the Angels were struggling and threatening to unravel. Tommy would have been ranting and raving,

screaming to the media, defending his actions, creating a deafen-
ing roar guaranteed to shake up everyone in the organization.
And maybe that might have worked.

But Scioscia did it differently. He did it his way, which is to
say he remained calm, never raising his voice, never complaining to the media. "If he had panicked, we probably would have,"
Salmon said. In the end, neither the manager nor the players did.

Picture Lasorda in the wild postgame celebration after
clinching the pennant. He would have been out in front, hugging
everybody, laughing and making speeches, accepting all media
interviews and personally directing everything that was going on
in the crazy clubhouse.

Again, Scioscia did it differently. Immediately after the Angels
clinched, he was nowhere to be found. Writers and broadcasters
looked and searched, but they couldn't find him. "I addressed the
players briefly, but I wanted it to be their time," he explained later.
"They were the ones responsible. They deserved the credit, and
I wanted them to enjoy it on their own."

Clearly, this is a man whose baseball thinking has been
shaped by more than a certain rotund former Dodgers manager.
"It wasn't just Tommy," Scioscia said. "There were a whole lot of
other people who helped give me my baseball foundation."

One of them, surprisingly, was waiter Alston, the manager who
immediately preceded Lasorda with the Dodgers. "He'd stepped
down in 1976, and my first spring training was 1977," Scioscia
said. "And Alston was working as a minor-league consultant. He
took a liking to me, for whatever reason. I remember he even came
to see me in Clinton, Iowa, and took me to lunch. Yeah, you could
say I was a little in awe of him. He had some great insights. He kept
telling me to just keep playing, that it's the same basic game."

Next up for this impressionable young catcher was a chance
to meet Roy Campanella. "Later, I realized how lucky I was to
get instruction from guys like Campy, Del Crandall, and John

Roseboro," Scioscia said. "Campy was incredible. He was this genuine human being who really cared about you. The support he gave you, you could feel it. It became a part of you. He was soft-spoken, but also one of the most powerful men I ever met."

Scioscia is a little like that, too. In many ways, he is an amalgam of some previous Angels managers. He is as serious a student of the game as Gene Mauch. He is as relaxed and media-friendly as the late Bill Rigney. And he is as knowledgeable and effective with a pitching staff as that other ex-catcher, Buck Rodgers.

"I try to be myself," Scioscia said. "The big thing is, you have to look at the strengths of your own club. You have to shape your team according to what you have. It's not something you can force if it's not there."

It was there, but it just happened to be hidden beneath the surface for the Angels in 2002.

It was their good fortune to find the right man to uncover it.

The Throwback

Darin Erstad is a throwback, with his high-stirrup socks and his roll-in-the-dirt, dive-headfirst, knock-your-helmet-off style. He is all intensity, all the time.

You could imagine him on those old Gashouse Gang teams in St. Louis, with Pepper Martin, Enos "Country" Slaughter and the guys, crashing into outfield walls and racing around the bases like some kind of banshee.

"The thing about Ersty is, he plays the same way the first day of spring training as he does in the seventh game of the World Series," said manager Mike Scioscia. "He doesn't know how to play any other way."

That's why the Angels are his team. He is their leader—on the field, in the clubhouse, on the bus going to the airport, it doesn't matter. He is the guy everyone else looks for, the one player who sets the tone.

In October, when this team was introduced to the excruciating pressure of the postseason for the very first time and wasn't sure exactly how to act, Erstad showed them. From the first game in the American League Division Series against the Yankees to the final World Series game against the Giants, he took over. He tied the record for most hits in the postseason (25) and, more than that, demonstrated to everyone the way to play.

"Who knows if you'll ever be back here again?" Erstad said. "Why not enjoy it? When you look back one day, do you want to say you were tight or tentative? Or do you want to know you enjoyed it?"

Erstad thought that was the easiest choice he'll ever have to make.

Darin Erstad watches his solo home run against Minnesota Twins pitcher Rick Reed in the first inning of Game 2 of the ALCS in Minneapolis. *AP/WWP*

"I leave it out on the field," he said.

Does he ever. If there was one October game that epitomized his postseason, it had to be Game 4 of the American League Championship Series against Minnesota.

It was a game that featured a flawless six-inning pitching duel between the Twins ace, Brad Radke, and the Angels remarkable rookie, John Lackey. The scoreless tension seemed to be building with each pitch and each out, until the bottom of the seventh inning.

That's when The Throwback took over. Erstad got a base hit, stole second, sprinted to third on a throwing error, and eventually scored the first run of the game. The Angels, taking their cue as usual from their fiery center fielder, then broke through with a flurry of base hits an inning later for an eventual 7-1 victory that put them one game—just one precious game—away from the World Series.

What made it highlight-reel stuff was the manner in which Erstad accomplished all of it. He appeared to have second base stolen after singling, but then the throw from catcher A. J. Pierzynski skipped past him into center field. There was only one problem. His helmet fell and covered his eyes. Erstad scrambled to his feet and began to race for third.

"I was lying on the ground and couldn't see the ball at first, but I heard the crowd and figured something had happened," he said. "But then my helmet fell down and I couldn't see third. So I knocked it off."

He finally scored the game's first run on a Troy Glaus single. An inning later, after singling again to kick-start the five-run explosion that put the game away, he took second on an errant pickoff throw from Johan Santana and again flung the helmet aside on his way.

It was as if he was signaling the Angels' new sign for clinching a victory. The old Boston Celtics had Red Auerbach lighting his cigar. The Angels now had Erstad tossing his helmet.

After the game, Erstad looked like a happy little kid who had been caught playing in the mud.

"I looked at him at one point tonight," said second baseman Adam Kennedy, "and he had grass stains from the top of his jersey to the bottom of his pants. This is what Darin has been waiting for all these years. He doesn't want to lose this opportunity. He's having a blast."

Angels fans were having a blast watching him. Erstad plays the game with a passion that is palpable. He careens around bases, smashes into walls, and grits his teeth so hard that you're afraid he's going to swallow his tobacco chew.

"The guy is unbelievable," Scioscia said. "I've never seen anyone play as hard as he does. He is wound tighter than anyone I've been around. I was on the 1988 Dodgers team with Kirk Gibson, and he was a great competitor. But I think Ersty plays at an even higher level than Kirk.

"And the thing is, the guy does it on every pitch, in every game. He practices as hard as he plays. Nobody is tougher on himself, either. Sometimes guys on our team worry when Ersty makes a mistake. I tell them if he didn't come in here between innings and hang himself, it must not have been that bad a mistake. Seriously, that's how hard he takes things."

For a while, it was difficult to know who the real Erstad was with the Angels. In his fourth year with the team, he dispensed the greatest individual season in franchise history, hitting .355, with 240 hits, 25 home runs, 121 runs, and 100 RBIs. It was the best offensive display by a major-league leadoff hitter ever.

But then one year later, bothered by a series of injuries and an emotional divorce, Erstad's average plummeted almost 100 points to .258. He didn't look or act like the same player, and heading into 2002, not everyone was sure which Erstad we'd see.

Soon enough, he showed us. If he wasn't back to that .355, once-in-a-lifetime flow, he settled in comfortably at the .280 to

.300 level, batting second behind David Eckstein and joining the little shortstop as the catalysts for a championship team. More importantly, he was back to his old slashing, sliding, head-first, running, full-bore style.

"I'm back to having fun again," he said. "People were wondering about me, and they had a right to do that. But I knew in my heart I wasn't that type of player."

His teammates knew it, too. They knew that nobody takes a loss harder than Erstad. Absolutely nobody.

"He hates losing, just hates it," said pitcher Jarrod Washburn. "He can go 0 for four, but if we win, he's happy. He makes you realize that's the way everyone should be."

And not surprisingly, that's the way everybody on this Angels team grew to be. They became a model for unselfishness because their leader showed them the way.

Nothing was more revealing about Erstad than the news that broke a month after the World Series. It seems he played most of the games against the Giants with a broken right hand that would require off-season surgery.

Considering that he hit .300 in the Series and had the huge leadoff home run in the bottom of the eighth inning of the surreal 6-5 comeback victory in Game 6, that would have seemed an astounding feat for most players—but not for Erstad. You could almost imagine him smiling about it and shrugging his shoulders later. "No big deal," he probably would have said of the injury. No, it undoubtedly wasn't—not for him.

Not for The Throwback.

The Good Soldier

For so many years he had carried them, through the pain and the frustrations and the disappointments. How appropriate, then, at the end of this surreal season, he would be the one carrying the symbol, the World Series championship trophy, parading around Edison Field with the glittering hardware above his head and a smile on his face as wide as the 10-gallon Gene Autry hat that eventually would be placed upon his head.

Tim Salmon, the ultimate good soldier, deserved this moment—maybe more than anyone else but the late "Cowboy" himself.

Salmon, the ten-year veteran who is the franchise leader in home runs (269) and RBIs (894), had witnessed most of the so-called hexes and curses at work. He'd seen Chuck Finley get his fluky injuries and Gary DiSarcina break his thumb in the heat of September. He'd been there when an 11-game August lead disappeared, and he's absorbed more strange front-office decisions than he'll ever admit.

But through it all, Salmon, who waited 1,388 games, longer than any current player in baseball, to make it to the postseason, has persevered. He was always the good soldier, the calming influence and the optimist as a new spring arrived.

And now he was being rewarded. The most consistent player in the history of this franchise was finally getting his chance. And he was planning to make the most of it.

"I tell these young guys now, 'Just appreciate it, man. Make the most of the moment,'" Salmon said. "That's the biggest thing . . . be aggressive. Don't go home thinking you left anything or held anything back."

Outfielder Tim Salmon laughs during a news conference before the division series against the Yankees.

Salmon didn't leave anything back in this golden October.

His amazing run started in Game 3 of the American League Division Series. The Yankees had powered their way to a deflating 6-1 lead, but the Angels, as has been their wont, kept pecking away at it, scoring one run here and two there and yet another and another to finally tie the score after seven innings. Then they inched one vulnerable run ahead in the bottom of the eighth.

That's when Salmon delivered his first big hit, off a Steve Karsay hanging curveball. He took a nice, controlled swing and sent the ball sailing high beyond the left-field fence for a two-run homer that not only put the lid on a breathtaking Angels comeback, but also sent the crowd at Edison Field into its first spasms of delight.

"I had goose bumps," the right fielder said after the 9-6 victory that set much of the tone for the rest of the playoffs. "I couldn't believe the crowd noise. You would have thought we'd won the seventh game of the World Series."

You didn't, Tim. But wait a few weeks—that will come later.

"This is what Angels fans had been waiting for all this time," Salmon said. "That was a lot of frustration they were letting out. I guess you dream about playing in games like this. And then you realize it's the Yankees. You're playing great baseball against the Yankees."

And it was almost like somebody scripted it. Of all the Angels to enjoy a moment like this one, nobody deserved it more than the 34-year-old Salmon. Year after year, he'd give you his 30 home runs and 90 to 100 RBIs. And year after year, something would happen to make him trudge home to Arizona disappointed and dejected. Now he was enjoying his postseason in the sun.

It was, as it turned out, just a start. The best was yet to come.

Who better, you would think later, to hit the home run to win the Angels' first-ever World Series game than Salmon? Who better to wait until that night, on that kind of nationally televised stage, to enjoy the game of his life?

In Game 2 of this Series, after the Angels had lost Game 1, Salmon would deliver four hits and not one, but two home runs, including the two-out, two-run shot in the bottom of the eighth—his favorite inning, apparently—to give the Angels a jaw-dropping 11-10 comeback victory.

"I've been joking with him that he's been looking like he's 12 years old in the playoffs," said Darin Erstad. "After he hit that last home run, he looked like he was eight."

For Salmon, it was sweet retribution. In Game 1, he had failed to deliver with David Eckstein on third base in a game the Angels wound up losing by one run. And he'd been brooding about it for the preceding twenty-four hours.

"It's in these games you want to be able to come through in the situations," he said. "Like I said, last night was a tough night. Tonight, I think just kind of getting that first hit out of the way helped things along."

It would not be his last big hit in a comeback victory. In Game 6, after the Angels had clawed back from a 5-0, potentially Series-ending deficit to make it 5-3, Salmon followed Erstad's leadoff homer in the eighth with a solid single of his own. When Garrett Anderson's slicing single was bobbled in left, Chone Figgins, who was running for Salmon, took third and Anderson raced to second. Both scored on Troy Glaus's ensuing double in a 6-5 victory many considered one of the great games in World Series history.

After it was all over in Game 7, after John Lackey and his steely-willed relievers subdued the Giants, 4-1, it was Salmon's time to celebrate, to let all those years of frustration come spilling out. He paraded around the field holding the trophy, then climbed onto the makeshift stage at second base and accepted Autry's cowboy hat, presented to him by Gene's wife, Jackie.

"It's all so amazing, so unbelievable, I can't even begin to describe my emotions," said Salmon, who was spritzing more champagne and soaking more of the bubbly all over his body than anyone else in the raucous Angels clubhouse afterward.

"I think," he said, "there's a lot of things I'm not going to really realize until later."

If nothing else, the veteran understood it was worth all the waiting, worth all the years of wondering what it would be like and how it would feel.

Tim Salmon now knew. And it was a feeling he was not likely to forget the rest of his life.

The Pest

It was Eric Chavez, Oakland's All-Star third baseman, who inadvertently coined the perfect nickname for David Eckstein.

"He's a real pest," Chavez said. "He's everywhere. They get a deflection or something, and he's always right there . . . He is always doing something to beat you."

For a long time, Eckstein was baseball's best-kept secret. A hidden treasure tucked into a little-noticed corner of Southern California—but not any more.

Not after the way he ignited the Angels to that stirring season, to that great run in the final months, and, finally, to their first world championship. He was the one at the top of the order and at the top of the popularity charts. The "X-Factor," announcer Rex Hudler called him, and fans at Edison Field showed their appreciation by raising their ThunderStix into the form of an "X" every time he came to the plate.

Eckstein is, by all accounts, the most unique player in baseball. He is a five-foot-six, 159-pound shortstop who could easily be mistaken for the batboy. "What is he?" sneered Toronto pitcher Ray Halladay, after Eckstein had beaten him with a home run. "About five foot two?"

Eck doesn't smoke or drink, although he broke down and took his first quick swig of alcohol in the pandemonium of the Angels clubhouse after the playoff-clinching victory in Texas.

"I did take a sip," Eckstein explained, "but only because the players made me."

On the road, Eck only leaves his hotel room to get something to eat. And even then, it is usually if there is a McDonald's close by. He drives a 1999 Nissan Maxima, and that's an upgrade from

David Eckstein, right, and Bengie Molina share a laugh during practice before Game 3 of the ALCS. *AP/WWP*

the 1994 Sentra he used to own until his father gave him the newer model.

He calls his father, Whitey, after every game, and his paychecks are shipped directly to his parents' home in Florida, where his mom is co-signed on his bank account.

"I told her she can take whatever she wants," Eckstein said.

Through all this, it is the Angels who take everything Eckstein gives. He is one of those intangible guys. An "Eddie Stanky–type," the old-timers say. Only Eck is more productive than the player they used to call "The Brat." How else do you explain the fact that he led the team in sacrifices, with 14, in being hit by pitches, with 27, and in grand slams, with three? That's right, this gnat of a man led not only the team, but the entire league in bases-loaded home runs, delivering two of them in back-to-back games.

But it certainly is not his power that makes him so valuable. It is his mind.

"Eck is the smartest player I've ever been around," said manager Mike Scioscia. "I know [Alex] Rodriguez and [Derek] Jeter are amazingly intelligent ballplayers. But I think Eck is smarter than both of them."

"He is the most fundamentally sound player I've ever seen," said Darin Erstad, the intense center fielder who enjoyed it two years ago when some of the players were kidding Eckstein and calling him Erstad's "Mini-Me."

Eckstein's specialties are all the little, subtle things that help you win baseball games. He will lay down a perfect squeeze bunt or take a 95-mph fastball somewhere on the body to get on base.

His base-running instincts are as good as any on the team, and he always seems to be in the right place at the right time on defense.

He runs full speed to first base when he is walked, the way Pete Rose used to in his prime. He also runs full speed from the dugout to his spot at shortstop before every inning. And none of it is fake; it is all genuine and born from a strict work ethic instilled by his parents.

"I come from a family where both my parents were teachers," Eckstein said. "They had five kids, and three of them had kidney transplants. I wasn't one of them, but, believe me, there were some tough times in our house."

Tough times that have helped mold this 28-year-old into a tough, hardened ballplayer who refused to believe the skeptics who kept saying he had no tools.

When he first showed up at the Angels spring-training camp after being plucked from the roster of the Boston Red Sox, few knew about him.

"To be honest," Scioscia said, "I'd never heard of him before we picked him up. He had a good spring for us, but what really started to sell us was how he handled tough situations. He was one cool cucumber out there."

The more Eckstein played—subbing for injured Adam Kennedy at second base that first spring—the more it became apparent the Angels needed him in the lineup. So Scioscia, with a serious nudge from infield coach Alfredo Griffin, started using him at shortstop. Then he moved him into the leadoff spot. And he's been there ever since.

Hitting leadoff is one of baseball's lost arts, but it is a role that Eckstein knew he'd fill one day, a role he studied and honed in the minor leagues.

"I had people sit me down early and talk to me about it," he said. "It made me change my approach at the plate. I started taking more pitches, letting teammates see what a pitcher has, things like that. I began to understand the thinking behind it."

Some close to the Angels were worried late in September when it appeared that Eckstein's body had worn down. He wasn't swinging the same or moving the same, and the Angels offense was suffering as a result.

"I think Eck was pretty much running on fumes there at the end," Scioscia said, knowing part of it was his fault. The manager considered his shortstop so valuable he couldn't risk taking him out of the lineup for the rest he so desperately needed.

Although Eckstein wound up hitting .293 for the season, he had been averaging .307 when he went into a 7-for-48 tail-spin that included a 0-for-21 stretch in the heat of September.

"I definitely didn't perform the way I wanted to the last two weeks of the season," Eckstein said, making it sound like it was all his fault. "It takes a lot out of you going down the stretch, especially trying to get in the way we were. Physically and mentally, I definitely think there was some strain. But that's still no excuse for the way I was hitting."

No apologies were necessary in the postseason. Eckstein hit .286 in the ALCS and .310 in the World Series. And every time the Twins or Giants looked up, there he was on the bases, setting the tone for an offense that never stopped scoring runs.

"The whole postseason experience was something I'll never forget," Eckstein said afterward. And Angels fans are not likely to forget the contributions of their extraordinary little shortstop.

Now they, and all of baseball, are beginning to understand the real value of David Eckstein. He isn't a five-tool player. He is a one-tool player.

It just so happens that in his case, the one tool is heart.

The Series MVP

It's hard to believe, but Troy Glaus actually had a disappointing 2002 regular season. No, he really did. Honest.

Even though he hit 30 home runs and finished with 111 RBIs, it is a measure of the potential the Angels, and everyone else in baseball, think this six-foot-five, 245-pound third baseman possesses. Anything less than the 88 combined home runs he delivered in the two previous seasons would be considered subpar.

"Troy's ceiling is amazing," said manager Mike Scioscia, knowing that only Alex Rodriguez hit more homers in the previous two-year span. "I think he has more upside than anybody else in this clubhouse."

That upside went through the roof in the postseason and especially in the World Series when the former UCLA star hit .385, with a team-high three home runs and eight RBIs, including the two go-ahead runs he drove in during the eighth inning of that theatric 6-5 come-from-behind victory over the Giants in Game 6.

"It's a great honor," Glaus said, holding onto the MVP trophy in the pandemonium following the Game 7 clincher. "But this is for the team, not for me. All twenty-five guys on this roster contributed to our winning."

He was right about that, but Glaus swung the biggest bat all the way through the postseason, pounding seven home runs in 16 playoff games. Even more significant was the way he did it, using the whole field and taking the outside pitches to right field—something he had refused to do for most of a frustrating regular season.

Troy Glaus lifts the MVP trophy above his head as he shares the honor with his teammates. *AP/WWP*

There was a point, in the middle of July, when people were beginning to wonder whether the right-handed-hitting Glaus was really going to be the next Mike Schmidt, or the next Dave Kingman. It was difficult to tell, the way he was failing to make contact on a regular basis. Inside, outside, it didn't matter where the pitch was. He was trying to jerk everything to left field. In 89 at-bats, he struck out 29 times, managing only one home run and averaging a puny .203. But if there was a problem with his swing, at least there was never anything wrong with his effort.

"He's got a great work ethic," said hitting coach Mickey Hatcher. "In fact, sometimes I have to get him to back off a bit. The thing is, he gets down on himself. He's been put in that category of a superstar, and it really hurts him when he feels he's not helping the team."

Glaus is probably more introverted than anyone on the club. And he tends to brood. His hesitancy to interact with the media doesn't help him much, either. But none of that seemed to matter once the Angels began playing in October.

He hit three home runs against the Yankees, including two in one game, then dispatched one of the biggest of the playoffs in Game 3 of the ALCS vs. Minnesota. The Angels and Twins were locked in a tense pitching duel when Glaus took an outside fastball from reliever J. C. Romero and powered it into the right-field bleachers to provide the winning margin in a 2-1 victory.

"It was a great piece of hitting, going the other way," said Twins catcher A. J. Pierzynski.

"It wasn't a great pitch, but it was a decent pitch. He got enough of it. Shoot, he swings a log. It looks like a 38-ounce bat."

Glaus's bat just kept looking bigger and bigger the deeper the Angels went into the postseason. When he does hit the ball to all fields, he is as intimidating a presence as anyone this side of Barry Bonds.

"A lot of it with Troy has been trying to get the idea where the pitch is going to be and stay in that zone," said hitting coach

Mickey Hatcher. "When Troy is seeing the ball good, he'll hit any-body. The more years he puts in, the more confidence he's going to get hitting to the right side. Then he's really going to be good."

When it comes to opposite field power, the only right-handed hitter in the sport who compares to Glaus is the Mets' Mike Piazza. But the difference in their games is that Piazza regularly goes the other way. Glaus only does it occasionally, although his timing was certainly right at the end of the season.

The former Pac-10 record holder for home runs hit eight balls out of the park in September. And then he maintained that momentum through the most important month of all.

"He went through a real tough stretch for a couple of months in the middle of the summer," Scioscia said. "But he stayed with it, kept working with it, was still driving in some key runs for us. Then he put it together later."

If you don't think Glaus has talent, just listen to the men who scout the American League. "He's stubborn and not the most coachable guy around," said one, who regularly tracks the Angels. "But when I rank guys on that team I'd like to have, he's still No. 1. Are you kidding me? With all the power and that arm, he's still got the best tools."

Glaus's presence in the middle of the Angels batting order makes a big difference, especially when he's in a home run groove. Most of the tough games the team lost a year ago were low-scoring events in which opponents homered and they didn't.

When Glaus is on a tear, they don't have to worry about that. At 26, this is still a young man who doesn't realize how gifted he is. Take, for example, that home run to right field that beat the Twins in Game 3 of the ALCS.

"Honestly, I didn't know it was gone until it hit the seats," Glaus said. "We've all played in [Edison Field] enough to know when it gets cold, the ball doesn't carry very well. For right-handers to go over [in right field], you've got to hit it pretty good."

When he connects, Glaus hits it better than pretty good. Now it will be interesting to see how capturing the World Series MVP trophy affects him. The Angels hope it bolsters his confidence and, above all, makes him realize that when he is hitting the ball to all fields, instead of trying to pull everything, he is a much more than just an effective hitter—he is a real force.

"I only wish I had his ability," said teammate Tim Salmon, who isn't too bad himself.

"Troy has got the best natural home-run swing I've ever seen. He has so much potential, it's almost scary."

The Last Angry Closer

The lasting image of the World Series the Angels never will forget is of Troy Percival standing on the mound, pumping his fists in exultation after throwing the pitch that Kenny Lofton hit harmlessly to center fielder Darin Erstad for the final out.

How appropriate that the man who had closed out so many pivotal games for the Angels through the years would come in to close out the biggest one yet.

Percy, as his teammates call him, has tossed 98-mph fastballs and a torrent of emotions through most of the major moments this franchise has experienced in recent years.

Call him the last angry closer—the Al Hrabosky or Goose Gossage of this kinder, gentler era. If his blurring fastballs don't freeze opposing hitters, that squinty, cold Clint Eastwood–like stare does.

Percival wears his attitude as proudly as he does that scruffy beard of his. He doesn't hold anything back, physically or emotionally. He just comes right at you, snarling with delight at the chance to throw his fearsome fastballs with the game hanging in the balance in the ninth inning.

"I'm so angry when I'm out there," Percival said. "And the thing is, I really don't know why. I'm sure people can see it. It's just the way I am. And when somebody gets a hit off me, I get angrier. But I try to control it. I think the anger helps my focus, actually."

That is the Percival the public sees. The closer who swaggers out of the bullpen amid wild applause in Anaheim. The amped right-hander who glares menacingly at the plate and intimidates everybody, except maybe the batboy—and you're not always so sure about him.

Closer Troy Percival reacts at the end of the Angels' 9-6 victory against the New York Yankees in Game 3 of the American League Division Series. *AP/WWP*

But the surprising thing about this intense man is that there are other, more subtle shades to any portrait you try to paint of him. He is the strong, if not always quiet, leader who can work a clubhouse or a dugout almost as effectively as he can mow down a collection of prominent power hitters.

He is the fanatically loyal, sensitive teammate and friend who never seems to forget the former players who helped get him where he is. He is the mentor who gladly takes aside some of the younger members of the Angels bullpen, teaching and guiding them and helping them understand what it means to be a big-league reliever.

And he is the devoted father who loves to hug his four-year-old son, Cole, and can't wait until he is old enough to bring him to the ballpark and join in the fun.

"On the field, when Percy comes in, he brings some serious intensity out there," said Erstad, who brings more than a bit of that himself. "What people don't know is that he sometimes comes into our dugout and changes the whole tone of things, too.

"Remember in Texas, when we were struggling to clinch [the wild card]? Well, Percy made it a point to come into the dugout a couple of innings before he was supposed to get ready to pitch. He said it was too tense in there. He just started screaming positive things, like 'Don't let them do this to you.' And you know, it was right about that inning when we busted loose and put the game away.

"He doesn't do that kind of thing very often. But when he does, you know he's there. His spirit is infectious."

Later that same day, in the middle of the champagne celebration in the visitor's clubhouse, it was Percival who was the first to remember an old friend who wasn't fortunate enough to be there.

"I was screaming for [Gary] DiSarcina," Percival said of the former Angels shortstop whose career was forced to end early because of injuries. "I saw Erstad, and I told him we had to call DiSar right away. He was so much a part of all this."

Erstad shook his head when he thought about it later. "I don't think anyone is more loyal or a better teammate than Percy," he said. But Percival doesn't take any credit for it.

"I'm not sure people understand," he said. "DiSarcina was the glue that held us together all those years, through the good and the bad. Guys like DiSar and [Chuck] Finley told me how to be a big-league player and taught me how to handle defeat."

Now it is Percival, the senior member of this pitching staff, who is doing the teaching. He is taking kids aside in the Angels bullpen and telling them what they need to do and how they have to do it to be successful at this level.

"Everyone feeds off his leadership," said Brendan Donnelly, the long-time minor-league reliever who was one of the happy surprises of this Angels championship run. "I know he's helped me a lot. He's given me a philosophy of how to pitch. He told me my stuff was good enough. Then he taught me how to use it. Out in the bullpen, we talk all the time about how to get out certain hitters. Well, that all starts with him. I can't say enough about his leadership."

Percival is only doing what Lee Smith, the great reliever who paused for a couple of years in Anaheim, did for him.

"He was fantastic to me," Percival said. "He taught me what was right and what was wrong. Now I try to do the same thing with our young guys. I want them to understand that when they come in with a big lead, they have to throw strikes. They have to go after it."

Percival always goes after it. It's not always pretty, and it's often nerve-wracking, the way it was when he put two runners on base and brought the potential tying run to the plate in that pressurized Game 7 against the Giants. But emotionally, you always know what you're going to get.

"That's who he is," pitching coach Bud Black said. "He's an emotional, aggressive fastball pitcher. I've only been out to the mound to talk to him a couple of times. But when you're out there, that look in his eyes definitely isn't the same one you see at four o'clock walking into the ballpark."

That look, maybe multiplied two or three times, is the one television viewers from around the country, who were previously unaccustomed to watching, had a chance to see close up and personal during the postseason. Percival saved two of the three Angels victories in the ALDS, two of the four in the ALCS, and three of the four in the World Series.

Through it all, he was the same angry, intense, frighteningly focused closer this team has had for the past eight years. Nothing bothers him; nothing makes him lose that famous concentration. Not even when the noise level at opposing ballparks reaches mind-blowing proportions the way it did in the ALCS in the Metrodome at Minnesota.

"I don't like putting up with all that noise when I'm sitting in the bullpen," Percival said. "But once I get into the game, it won't bother me."

Nothing bothers him. Not with that stare. Not with that anger. Not with that attitude.

When Troy Percival is on the mound, even the noise seems intimidated.

The Pure Hitter

The swing is so perfect it drives Darin Erstad crazy.

"G. A. puts the same swing on the ball every time," said the Angels center fielder. "He makes it look so damn easy. And me, I'm scuffling and struggling and changing my swing almost every time out there. Then I look up and G. A.'s swing is so smooth and perfect every time. It makes me nuts."

It doesn't do much for the composure of opposing pitchers, either.

Garret Anderson is the best pure hitter on the Angels roster and one of the best in all of baseball. But his hitting ability is like the rest of Anderson's game. It almost comes too matter-of-factly. He is as unassuming as he is consistent and as languid as he is proficient.

What he proved in the World Series is that he is the anti–Barry Bonds—the polar opposite of the spectacular but arrogant left fielder of the San Francisco Giants.

"I understand why Bonds is getting so much more attention," Anderson said. "He's done a lot more than I have. He deserves it. And besides, I'm not a very flashy person. I play hard and let my numbers do the talking."

Most of the time, they speak volumes. Writers covering the Angels' first World Series were amazed to discover that the *other* left fielder—the one playing for Anaheim—had hit 83 home runs and driven in 363 runs across the previous three seasons. And yet the knock on the clear MVP of the Angels' 2002 season is that he isn't aggressive enough. He won't dive for balls in the outfield. He won't always run every ball out full speed.

Outfielder Garret Anderson watches the flight of his solo home run against the Twins in the second inning of Game 3 of the ALCS. *AP/WWP*

"He's so misunderstood," said manager Mike Scioscia. "I've said all along that G. A. is the best athlete on the team. He has a burning desire to compete like the others, but with him it just doesn't always come to the surface. He could be great at any sport. You put a basketball in his hand, and he'd play at a high level. And if he played football, he'd be a great wide receiver."

In his first All-Star season, Anderson tied Boston's Nomar Garciaparra for the major-league lead in doubles with 56. He finished second, behind the Yankees' Alfonso Soriano, with 88 extra-base hits. His 123 RBIs ranked him fourth in the American League, and his .306 average was the 10th best in the league.

"I'd like to think a few people are looking at my bio this week and saying, 'Wow!'" Anderson said during the World Series. "I think some writers definitely will be surprised. But for me, when it comes to personal attention, I don't care. I can take it or leave it. I don't hide from the media. But I'm not a small-talk guy."

Anderson always has been quiet, even through the early years in Anaheim, when his name was always mentioned in Angels trade rumors. Anderson-for-this-guy, Anderson-for-that-guy—every winter, it was the same story line.

"I'm proud of him, because G. A. withstood all that," said teammate Tim Salmon. "He's lived through it and gotten better."

Maturity helped, too. When he first came up, Anderson was viewed as a potential high-average hitter with below-average power. But as he grew older and became more comfortable at the plate, he began turning on the ball and developed into a steady home-run threat.

"I used to ask guys what kind of hitter they thought I'd be, and they used to say someone who would hit in the No. 3 hole or the No. 5 hole," Anderson said. "Now, here I am hitting cleanup. And I like it. I welcome being in position to drive in runs. It's fun being in that position all the time."

If his hits are impressive, his durability deserves almost equal mention. His teammates talk all the time about his penchant for avoiding injuries.

"The guy answers the bell every night," said Angels coach Joe Maddon. "I don't know if people understand how important that is across a full season. He is almost disgustingly consistent."

He is a far better outfielder than people think, too. He made a couple of great plays in the postseason, including a running, stretching, one-handed catch in the left-field corner in Game 2 against the Yankees that was so similar to Sandy Amoros's legendary grab in the seventh game of the 1955 World Series for the Dodgers that it was almost eerie.

"I think he's the best left fielder in the game, and people don't realize it," Maddon said. "You always hear all that stuff about him not getting dirty. Well, you know why that is? It's because he positions himself so well and he studies hitters so much, he doesn't have to leave his feet."

In a way, his World Series performance best exemplified Anderson. He'd had a relatively quiet first six games, delivering a clutch hit here and there, but nothing particularly exceptional— until the seventh game, until the moment when it was most needed.

Anderson strolled to the plate with the bases loaded in the bottom of the third inning, with the outcome still very much in doubt. And with that familiar swing—that smooth, almost text-book stroke—he crushed a line drive that whistled just fair down the right-field line. All three runners scored, and Anderson stood at second base, a hint of a smile playing at the corner of his lips. He'd done what he'd been doing all year long. He'd delivered the big hit in the biggest game of them all.

"I knew he'd have a good at-bat in that situation," Maddon said. "I think he'd been trying too hard to come up with the big hit before. But he sure did it at the most important time, didn't he?"

He sure did. He delivered the same way in the ALDS, when he proved even to the hardened critics in New York that, as left fielders go, he's not exactly Carnegie Deli chopped liver.

"I think he is by far the most underrated player in baseball," Erstad said. "He's one of the finest pure hitters in the game. You hear that around the American League all the time. Guys are always saying his swing is almost perfect. He hits the ball harder [and] more consistently than anyone on our team. And I think he'd rank in the top five in our league in that category."

Maybe the best time to watch Anderson is in the first few days of spring training, when everyone else is rusty and out of sync. It is there, in the warm sunlight of Arizona, that only one Angels player can move into the batting cage and immediately begin swinging the way he did on the final day of the previous season.

Without the loud crowds and the reverberating ThunderStix, you can close your eyes and listen closely to the sound of the ball hitting Garret Anderson's bat. You hear it and you nod your head in instant recognition.

Ah, yes, you think. Even the sound is almost perfect.

The New Ace

When Chuck Finley left the Angels in 2000, there was a huge vacuum. Suddenly, there was no one there to lead the pitching staff, to accept the responsibility, to hold the unofficial, but well-deserved title of staff ace.

Then up stepped Jarrod Washburn to fill the left-handed void.

"It doesn't bother me if they want to call me an ace," said the 28-year-old Washburn before the 2002 season. "I don't know if you can do that with this staff, because we have five guys that are worthy. If I'm tabbed as the guy, I'll look forward to the challenge."

One year later, there is no longer any question about his status. After he won 18 games, including 12 in a row at one point, and finished with a 3.15 earned run average, Washburn clearly earned the team's No. 1 pitching slot.

"It's perfect for Wash," said outfielder Darin Erstad. "He is a fierce competitor who wants to be challenged by the biggest, toughest situation out there. He will love this."

Pitching coach Bud Black concurs. To him, an ace is the guy who wants the challenge. It is someone who understands that the escalating pressure is part of the job. When it is the rubber game of a big series, your ace is the pitcher who can't wait to get out there.

"He always wants the ball in big games," Black said. "Some guys don't. Wash does."

Fellow coach Joe Maddon senses the same thing. "Jarrod's got broad shoulders," Maddon said. "He's got the personality to do it. I think Washburn can be that kind of figure for our pitching staff, not only because of his ability but because of what's inside him."

Starting pitcher Jarrod Washburn reacts after the Giants' David Bell flew out to end the top of the fourth inning with the bases loaded in Game 1 of the World Series. *AP/WWP*

Washburn is unusual in that his "out" pitch is a fastball that registers only 90 or 91 mph on the radar gun, but reacts more like a 98-mph heater in the strike zone.

"He can make a fastball hop like you would see from a guy who throws 98," said veteran Kevin Appier. "It looks like it's rising. It's all the things his fastball does. It cuts, sinks, hops. And he's not even done yet. It just does wicked things coming out of his hand. And then the thing that separates Wash is that he acts and pitches like he's been around for more years than he actually has. He just has a better idea of what it's all about than most guys his age."

While most pitchers have two weapons scouts call "plus-pitches," Washburn really only has one. There are games when he seems to throw 95 percent fastballs.

"He has a gift," said fellow Angels pitcher Scott Schoeneweis. "Very few people can throw 120 fastballs a game and win. He's got a real good idea of how to use his fastball and change speeds. I know there are batters that walk back and shake their heads, like, how did that guy get me out? He has such confidence that he doesn't care. He's not afraid. He's coming with his No. 1 pitch. He knows it. The hitter knows it. Everybody in the ballpark knows it. He's still successful. That says a lot about him."

There is a grittiness to Washburn, too. If he gets hit hard early, he doesn't let it bother him. He will continue to compete, something not all the other pitchers on the Angels staff find easy to do.

"He's a lot like Finley that way" said closer Troy Percival. "If he gets into trouble early he'll pitch his way out of it, and the next thing you know it's the seventh inning and he's still out there. That's a big benefit for him. He's got the mentality you need to be a No. 1 starter."

He has the personality too. Washburn isn't one of those smoldering, intense types who hides in the trainer's room. He is the gregarious guy who is always in the middle of every locker room activity, whether it's organizing a team fishing trip on the road or masterminding the clubhouse NCAA basketball tournament pool.

He has become a media favorite, as well He likes being quoted and enjoys the fact that he is developing into one of the team's spokesmen. Sometimes, of course, that can get him in trouble. Like the time in 2001 when he noticed that future furry star, the rally monkey, was drawing considerable attention on the scoreboard.

"Maybe if they worked as hard promoting the team as they did the monkey, we wouldn't have to play in front of 15,000 fans," Washburn said. When the rally monkey developed into a full-fledged superstar this past season, Washburn, to his credit, seemed to take note. "I have no further comment on the monkey," he said, grinning.

"He's a personable guy," said pitching coach Bud Black. "He's genuine. He reminds me of a position player who pitches. If you equate it to football, there are offensive linemen who like their quarterback and there are offensive linemen who don't like their quarterback. Our offensive line loves Washburn."

What's not to love? His 12-game winning streak a year ago was matched only by Houston's Wade Miller. No one else in the major leagues put together more victories in a row—not Pedro Martinez, not Curt Schilling, not even Randy Johnson.

The opposition noticed. "Not everyone can pitch up *here*," said Oakland third baseman Eric Chavez, drawing a line with his hand through the top of his shoulders, "and get away with it. When he gets you, you know why. He's got good stuff."

Minnesota center fielder Torii Hunter said Washburn's fastball "explodes." Then he added: "He's pretty special."

If there is one lingering question about Washburn, it is his stamina. He hadn't stayed healthy for an entire season until last year. And in October, he was more tired and, as a result, more inconsistent than he would have preferred in the postseason.

"Staying healthy an entire season is one of the big keys for me," Washburn said. "It's a goal I've set for myself. I felt physically better this past year than I had ever felt before."

The next goal will be to win 20 games. He was only two shy in 2002. If confidence has anything to do with it, Washburn has a big chance.

"Jarrod's a confident guy and had enough success to recognize he belongs here and could be a major contributor," general manager Bill Stoneman said. "Everyone knows he's very competitive and determined, and shows everybody by example how to go about the business of playing baseball. His confidence really shows."

Washburn's biggest asset is his knack for winning. He already has the highest winning percentage in Angels history for any pitcher with more than 50 decisions. At 46-26, his .639 percentage is the only one above .600 and considerably better than the next two pitchers on the list, Bert Blyleven at .579 and Frank Tanana at .576.

"It's a big thing for me," Washburn said. "I don't like to lose."

Not many aces do.

The Rockin' First Baseman

He is the hip first baseman who plays in a rock band called Sand-frog in the off season and dyed his hair bright Angels red during the postseason. He is smiling and friendly and often overlooked in a clubhouse full of higher-profile, more intense players like Darin Erstad and Troy Percival.

But for a guy who was supposed to start the season platooning at first base, Scott Spiezio certainly made his presence felt during 2002.

First, it was with his glove. The glove that speared potential doubles scalded down the right field line and smothered ground balls that looked like sure singles between first and second base. The same glove that scooped throws in the dirt easier than your neighborhood teenager scoops Jamoca Almond Fudge at Baskin-Robbins.

"He saves a ton of runs for us," said pitcher Jarrod Washburn. "I don't know if you can count how many runs he's saved this season. He seems to make some kind of diving play three or four times a game. I definitely haven't seen a better-fielding first baseman in the league this year."

The Angels, to a man, thought Spiezio was robbed of the American League Gold Glove award that went to Seattle's John Olerud. The Mariners first baseman is admittedly a fine fielder and much more of a prototype at the position because he is tall and left-handed. But Spiezio, at a slightly baggy six foot two, 225 pounds, doesn't have to apologize to anybody when it comes to making plays—especially spectacular plays. He finished the season with a .997 fielding percentage. Olerud's percentage was .996.

If his glove drew most of the attention during the regular season, it was Spiezio's bat—the one he swings as easily as he

First baseman Scott Spiezio smiles during workouts before the World Series. As evidence of his wild streak and team spirit, Spiezio dyed his facial hair bright red for Game 1. *AP/WWP*

plays that guitar of his—that jarred him into the spotlight in the postseason. On a team full of disciplined contact hitters, Spiezio was the most dependable when it came to driving in runs. He finished with 19 to tie Sandy Alomar's major-league postseason record, accomplished with Cleveland in 1997. He also tied Marty Barrett's record set in 1986 for highest average with runners in scoring position at .688 (11 for 16).

And the Angels might not have had a more important hit than the three-run home run Spiezio lifted into the right-field seats in the seventh inning to begin the miracle comeback from a 5-0 deficit that resulted in the 6-5 victory in Game 6 of the World Series. In the seven games vs. San Francisco, Spiezio finished with eight RBIs, the same as Troy Glaus, the Series MVP.

"I was just looking to keep the ball on a line and drive in runs," Spiezio said. "That's been my philosophy most of the season, just try to keep the ball out of the air. If I happen to get one up and it carries out, that's a bonus. But I'm looking to keep it on a line."

The Angels were looking to just keep the good vibes rolling from this first baseman who wasn't even in their full-time plans when the season started. It is funny how those things sometimes work out. Team officials considered Spiezio more of a valuable utility player until Mo Vaughn, the slugger who was supposed to light up their offense, fizzled faster than California's electric power sources.

When Vaughn was traded to the Mets for pitcher Kevin Appier over the winter, manager Mike Scioscia looked around and decided the switch-hitting Spiezio might not be a bad fit at first base—at least against right-handed pitching.

The plan, going into spring training, was to platoon him with right-handed-hitting Shawn Wooten. But then Wooten tore ligaments in his thumb early in Arizona. Spiezio not only continued to make eye-popping plays on defense, but he started crushing left-handed pitching. "It's something that I knew if I got the opportunity I thought I'd be better with more consistent at-bats," Spiezio said. "Coming into spring training, I didn't know what it was going to be like."

By the time Wooten returned to the active roster in the second half of the season, Spiezio was established as the full-time first baseman. Wooten, a terrific hitter, was platooned as the DH with Brad Fullmer. "The opportunity has been awesome," Spiezio said. "I think Shawn getting hurt opened the door for me to hit off lefties. It was unfortunate for him, but it was probably the reason that I got to hit off the lefties."

Of such strange circumstances are pennant-winning and World Series championship teams forged. At least playing in games of postseason magnitude was no big thing to Spiezio. His father, former big-league third baseman Ed Spiezio, had been preparing him for that kind of pressure all his life.

"He'd pitch me batting practice every day," Spiezio said of his dad, "and we'd always end it with a situation where I'd be in the World Series. I think that's the reason I feel comfortable here, because I've done that in my head so many times as I grew up."

Maybe just as important was the way Spiezio fit into Scioscia's "little ball" philosophy of advancing runners, getting people in scoring position and driving in runs with or without base hits. Maybe no one on this team grasped the full concept as well as the guitar-playing first baseman.

"Sometimes getting them in means hitting a ground ball to second or managing a sac fly or a squeeze bunt," Spiezio said. "Every guy on this team can do just about everything, and that's why we're able to score a lot of runs."

If Spiezio isn't the Angels' most valuable player, he might have been their most surprising. "I don't think anybody on our team expected what Spiez has done for this club," said hitting coach Mickey Hatcher. "And it's not just his RBIs, either. He's saved us so many runs with his glove. The players just love him. And the infielders really love him because he picks so many balls out of the dirt."

Angels fans grew to love him even more in the playoffs and World Series, when every time they looked up, he seemed to be driving in a pivotal run. "He's cut down on [trying to hit] home runs to become a big RBI guy," Hatcher said. "I think playing every day has got him into a groove."

Groove or not, the Angels didn't care. They just wanted their hip new first baseman to keep on rockin'.

The Sudden Hero

One day he was quietly doing his job, grinding away in the shadows, the most improved and maybe least appreciated player on the team.

The next day, Adam Kennedy was a hero bordering on a legend.

That's what happens when you hit not one, not two, but three home runs in a single ALCS game. The less-than-muscular Kennedy, who had homered only seven times in the entire regular season, suddenly made like Barry Bonds in Game 5 against Minnesota.

"It was pretty amazing," said Kennedy.

No, it was more than that. It was the jaw-dropping climax to the rally that finally put the Angels into the World Series after a forty-one-year wait. It was one of those completely unexpected, out-of-left-field postseason performances that we've seen, not surprisingly, from so many other second basemen in the past, from the Billy Martins to the Bill Mazeroskis to the Bobby Richardsons to the Mark Lemkes—the second-banana second baseman who rises up to be the surprise hero.

This is how far out of the blue Kennedy's game was: after he'd already hit two home runs, he came up in the seventh inning; catcher Bengie Molina had singled, and manager Mike Scioscia ordered him to *bunt*?

That's right. Scioscia, ever the "little ball" advocate, flashed him the bunt sign. Kennedy saw it, never flinched and tried his best to comply. But he fouled off the pitch from Twins reliever Johan Santana, instead. So Scisocia shrugged and took off the bunt sign.

Adam Kennedy rounds the bases after hitting his second home run of the game, a solo shot in the fifth inning of Game 5 of the ALCS against the Minnesota Twins in Anaheim. *AP/WWP*

That's how, on an 0-2 count, Santana hung a curveball, and Kennedy took his usual long uppercut of a swing and drove the ball into the right-center-field bleachers for home run No. 3 to put his team ahead, 6-5, and ignite a series-clinching 10-run burst.

After hitting only 23 career homers in 1,652 at-bats, he had belted his third in just four at-bats that day. The Angels' red-clad crowd—still not ready to fully believe at the start of this series—suddenly went bonkers. If there was one hit in the postseason that made everyone realize that this team and this story line was for real, this was it.

And just like that, Kennedy was brushing shoulders in the baseball history books with the likes of Reggie Jackson, George Brett, Bob Robertson, and this other guy they called The Babe. They were the only other four players to deliver three home runs in a postseason game.

If it was a performance for the ages, it was also a fitting cap to Kennedy's season. He was, after all, the No. 9 hitter who wound up with the leading batting average (.312) on a team full of guys famous for spraying line drives in all directions. The second baseman, who had been platooned with Benji Gill for most of the regular season, warmed up to hit .407 in August, second best in the majors next to none other than Barry Bonds. He raised his average against left-handers from .242 in 2001 to .275 in 2002. He averaged .357 in the ALCS and, to hardly anyone's surprise, was named the series MVP. Then he went out and hit a solid .280 in the World Series.

"I just plug along and try to help," Kennedy said at one point. "I'm just a regular player." No, he *was* just a regular player. After that three-homer burst, his name will be forever etched in the neon-like lights of every Angels fan's memory.

"Kennedy for President," read several of the signs at Edison Field where, a few days later, the World Series would begin. The man who had been almost anonymous for most of the regular season looked at them, shook his head, and smiled. "It's just unbelievable," he said.

More than his offense, it was Kennedy's defense that convinced the Angels to reward him with a new, one-year, $2.27 million contract for this season. Throughout spring training, Kennedy and workaholic shortstop David Eckstein put in long hours with infield coach Alfred Griffin, perfecting their timing and their footwork around second base.

"I can't remember anyone on the team working any harder than those two did in the spring," Scioscia said.

And the work paid off. Kennedy went from a liability to a Gold Glove candidate in the field, smoothly turning double plays and going deep behind the bag to make spectacular, off-balance plays.

Of course, he had some good teachers. His locker is next to Darin Erstad's, and Kennedy has said repeatedly that he learned how to play the game from watching the center fielder who never takes a play off.

In the end, Kennedy's huge Game 5 was characteristic of this team that squeezed everything out of every man on the roster on the way to that amazing championship run.

"That's what we're all about," said first baseman Scott Spiezio. "Getting guys you don't expect to contribute. Like A. K. coming out and hitting three home runs in a game like that. You don't expect it, but he did it."

A few months earlier, in the spring of 2002, longtime Angels watchers were already projecting that Eckstein, who is not a natural shortstop, would move over to second base in 2003, making room for one of the franchise's top prospects, Alfredo Amazega, at short. Kennedy, they figured, would be the odd man out.

A year later, no one is thinking that way. "Adam was a key part of our success last season," said general manager Bill Stoneman. "His postseason performance reinforced the quality of player we believe Adam to be."

It also renewed Kennedy's belief that, as a former All-American at Cal State Northridge, his potential still hasn't been fully tapped. "You definitely want to be put in a class of second basemen," Kennedy said, after signing his new contract. "You want to be closer to guys like Bret Boone, Jeff Kent, and Roberto Alomar. You want to keep going up the ladder."

The fact that all his extra work paid dividends didn't go unnoticed by Kennedy, either. "I enjoy working out more," he said. "I feel so much more comfortable with the confidence I've gained. Last offseason, I had so many doubts. It's making a big difference this offseason. I know what to do, and I know that I can do it."

After three home runs in one postseason game, the whole world now knows.

The Phenom

They don't come along very often—the young ones with skills polished beyond their years—but when they do, they remain embedded in your baseball consciousness. A Mantle, a Mays, a Gooden, a Jeter, an A-Rod.

And now a K-Rod.

Francisco Rodriguez flashed across the cool October sky like some rocket they were testing at Vandenberg Air Force Base. His appearance, at the tender age of 20, was so unexpected and so dazzling that he was flooded with nicknames. They called him "Frankie" or "K-Rod" or "Secret Weapon." Or, as his teammate Tim Salmon simply preferred to call him, "The Phenom."

He was all that and a little more. "He was our gift from God," said Angels coach Mickey Hatcher. And to think only a few months before, he'd been an unknown minor leaguer struggling to establish himself as a starting pitcher, accumulating a disappointing 11–12 record that was making some in the Anaheim organization wonder if he had much of a future.

Then someone had the bright idea to switch him to the bullpen. It was as if a sudden bolt of lightning had reverberated its way through the heart of this franchise. Working in relief, Rodriguez was a revelation, blazing through Double A and Triple A—striking out 120 hitters in 83⅓ innings. The more he flourished, the more the Angels flirted with the idea of calling him up after the triple-A playoffs ended in mid-September. Why not, they figured. Why not have a look at this kid and see whether he might be able to help them in 2003?

What they and everyone else saw was almost too much to comprehend. Frankie came up and registered 13 strikeouts in

Relief pitcher Frankie Rodriguez showed his maturity and mettle during the 2002 postseason, and the Angels will certainly look to him to contribute in 2003. *AP/WWP*

five and two-thirds scoreless innings in five games against the Oakland Athletics, Seattle Mariners, and Texas Rangers. Manager Mike Scioscia and pitching coach Bud Black looked at each other more than once and tried not to smile.

"We liked his composure, his mound presence, his stuff," Black said. "We began to think that, hey, maybe this guy can help us in the postseason. Maybe he can have a real impact."

Rodriguez never seemed to have any doubt. This kid was as cool as an iced margarita glass.

Lots of rookies have come in and made a quick postseason splash, but few have ever done it with the style and the dominance of Frankie—even if he did think he blew his chance in the second game of the ALDS against the Yankees. Brought in by Scioscia to hold a 4-3 lead in the sixth inning, he made his first major mistake since being called up to the big leagues. He hung an 0-2 slider to Alfonso Soriano and the Yankees second baseman hit a two-run homer.

Lots of managers would have sat the rookie down at that point. Scioscia didn't. He left him in, and Frankie retired Jason Giambi, Bernie Williams, and Robin Ventura in order in the next inning. He wound up the winning pitcher when the Angels rallied for three runs in the eighth in an 8-6 victory.

But that was just the warmup for Rodriguez. By the time his wild postseason ride had ended, by the time his 94-mph fastball and that slider with more bite to it than a Louisiana gator had made some of baseballs best hitters look foolish, he had worked in 11 of the Angels' 16 games. He won five of them, tying Randy Johnson's major-league record, and absorbed just one loss. He faced 70 batters overall, striking out 28. He allowed just five runs.

"The kid is amazing," said Black. "The closest thing I'd seen to him was Bret Saberhagen when he came up with Kansas City at age 20 in the mid-1980s. The only difference was that Saby had a looseness to him, yet he was always focused during the game. Frankie has a calm to him, but you see more intensity. I think his confidence is something that's inherent when you're young. But it's part of his personality, too. He is very confident in his ability."

His presence in the Angels clubhouse was remarkable. He was part cocky and yet very humble at the same time. After he'd been successful in the ALDS and ALCS, he still hadn't faced the challenge of a World Series. He was standing in front of his cubicle the day before Game 1 when he was approached and asked if he didn't feel a little nervous about the whole thing.

"Did I look nervous in the playoffs?" Frankie asked.

"No," he was told.

"Exactly," he said. "I'm not going to war. I'm just playing baseball."

And yet, if the performance side didn't worry him, the very idea that he was there, in the major leagues, was still mind-boggling to him. He said he had felt blessed to be called up to Triple A Salt Lake City at midseason.

"I figure I go to Triple A, and I finish strong with some good numbers and maybe I have a chance to make the big club in spring training next year," he said. "I never thought I'd go to the big leagues this year. Then I make the roster for the playoffs and I'm out there pitching. It is something really amazing. This opportunity, it comes one time in a lifetime. Sometimes, I wonder, am I dreaming or not?"

He was not. He was there, and not only pitching, but over-powering hitters.

"It's one thing to have the tools at that age," said Salmon, who dressed in the cubicle next to Frankie. "It's another thing to be playing in the postseason and the World Series in front of screaming crowds of 45,000 or 50,000 people. I mean, when I was 20, I don't think I could have stood up in front of my classmates in school."

The oldest of thirteen brothers and sisters raised by his grandmother and grandfather in Caracas, Venezuela, Frankie had to learn early in life to fend for himself. "My mother and father weren't involved," he said. As the big brother in a family that size, you tend to mature early. But once he signed with the Angels for $900,000, his baseball maturity didn't kick in until he made that now-famous switch from a starting pitcher to a reliever.

"Right away I liked it," he said. "For me, it was way better. As a starting pitcher, you've got to concentrate for six or seven innings, trying to pitch a complete game. In the bullpen, as a setup man or closer, you usually only have to face two or three hitters. You can be more aggressive this way. A starting pitcher has to have a fastball, a change-up, a curve, and maybe a sinker. I just throw a fastball and a slider."

Right. And Kobe Bryant only concentrates on jumpers and dunks.

The key for Rodriguez is that his pitches are the same he's always thrown. He doesn't have to work to get that extraodinary break to his slider. It comes naturally to him. "I don't really throw a slider," he said. "I just change my arm angle. If I release the ball at a three-quarter angle, it moves like a slider. If I throw over the top, it breaks straight down."

The Role Players

In a way, it is deceiving to identify any of the 2002 Angels as role players. Because when you look at them as a whole, that's what they all were. Each played his role to near perfection.

Some, though, were less publicized than others. Especially at the end, in the rush to anoint the emerging stars who took them to the world championship, it was easy to overlook so many of the others who quietly made huge contributions.

It began with the pitching staff, with the addition of the two veteran starters who stabilized the rotation, Kevin Appier and Aaron Sele. Talk to those on the team and they will tell you that when the offseason trade was made, sending Mo Vaughn to the Mets for Appier, and then the huge $24 million multiyear signing of Sele was made official, that was the start. That was the point at which many players on the club felt they had a chance.

They were right. Between them, Appier and Sele won a modest 22 games, but their presence helped alleviate the pressure on a young staff, allowing not only the maturation of the future ace, Jarrod Washburn, but also the accelerated improvement of Ramon Ortiz, who finished with 15 victories. By the time John Lackey arrived later in the summer, this was already a good staff. The tall, lanky rookie from Texas made it even better, taking over as the No. 5 starter, working the wild card–clinching victory in Texas and going on to pitch brilliantly in the postseason, topped off, of course, by his victory in Game 7 of the World Series, the first time a rookie has accomplished that feat in 93 years.

Now, that is a real role player. But there was more. There was Bengie Molina, the catcher who won a Gold Glove and expertly guided the Angels pitching staff through its first emotional pennant race and postseason. A devoted student of manager Mike Scioscia, the former All-Star catcher for the Dodgers, Molina didn't overwhelm anyone offensively (.245 with five homers and 47 RBIs), but he was the steady leader behind the plate, with soothing words and a strong arm, that all good teams need in order to win. And when Bengie slowed down, the Angels called up his brother, Jose, to fill in, and several Angels pitchers gave Jose the ultimate compliment: they couldn't tell the difference when he was catching. Jose always smiled whenever they told him that.

The role playing didn't stop there, either. Brad Fullmer arrived as a free agent and immediately stabilized the DH position. Then there was Orlando Palmeiro, the fourth outfielder who filled in wherever needed. All he did was hit a steady .300 and always manage to get his bat on the ball (only 22 strikeouts in 263 at-bats).

Benji Gil, who platooned much of the season with Adam Kennedy at second base, was another handy guy to have around, especially since he could play any position in the infield. Although sometimes sitting out for long stretches, Gil always seemed to contribute when called upon. He hit .285 in the regular season, and in just five World Series at-bats, he collected four timely hits.

On the mound Ben Weber (7-2, 2.54), Scott Schoeneweis (9-8, 4.88), and Scot Shields (5-3, 2.20) all proved invaluable members of Scioscia's bullpen. And in Schoeneweis's case, a classic example of a player who was willing to give up his starting spot without complaining as long as he knew it helped the team. Desperately in need of a left-hander out of the bullpen, Scioscia converted Schoeneweis from a starter into a reliever. And especially when Lackey arrived, it only helped to make the Angels a better-balanced, stronger club.

But if there were two role players who best epitomized the remarkable chemistry on this Angels team, they were Shawn Wooten and Brendan Donnelly—two baseball vagabonds who kicked around the game for years, wondering if their chance would ever come. And then, in one magic, Orange County summer, opportunity arrived for both.

Wooten is the DH from Moose Jaw. That's the Canadian town in Saskatchewan where he spent part of two seasons, wondering some nights if they'd have enough bats and balls to finish the game. Originally drafted by the Phillies, Wooten also made stops in such major metropolitan cities as Bristol, Connecticut, Fayetteville, Arkansas, Lakeland, Florida, and Cedar Rapids, Iowa. Moose Jaw was his favorite, though.

"Don't knock it," Wooten said. "Some nights, we had as many as 3,500 people in the stands, which isn't bad for a hockey town."

Wooten landed with the Angels two years ago, as a 28-year-old rookie, and he hit .312, driving in a respectable 32 runs in just 79 games. He was scheduled to be the right-handed platoon first baseman, alternating with Scott Spiezio, when the 2002 season started. But he tore ligaments in his thumb and didn't return until late in the summer.

Still, that didn't stop Wooten from contributing. He hit .292 with 19 RBIs in just 113 at-bats as the right-handed DH. Then, in the postseason, he became a big-time run producer, highlighted by his three hits, including the home run that ignited the 9-5, series-clinching victory against the Yankees in Game 4 of the ALDS. The only thing better than his timely bat was the disbelieving look on his face in the raucous Angels clubhouse afterward.

From Moose Jaw to slackjaw, you could call it. There was no longer any doubt that Wooten belonged.

Donnelly's story was, in many ways, even more amazing. He has had more minor-league disappointments than most athletes could have endured: drafted by the White Sox in the 27th round in 1992; released in April of 1993; signed by the Cubs in June of that year; released in March of 1994; signed by an independent league team in Parkersburg, West Virginia, but pitched only 10 times;

signed by Cincinnati in March 1995, stayed four years, mostly in Double A; signed with Tampa Bay to pitch Triple A in May, 1999; released August 12; signed with Pittsburgh in August of the same year, worked two games in Double A and then was released a week later; signed with Toronto a few days later and worked at Triple A, only to be released in July of 2000; signed with the Cubs in August of 2000, where he didn't pitch well in Triple A and didn't get many breaks.

But that's OK. His biggest break was yet to come. In January of 2001, the Angels called. He went 9-2 in Double A and Triple A, striking out 50 in 41⅓ innings at Salt Lake. He was called up to the big club in April, sent back down, and then came up for good in June.

Scioscia and pitching coach Bud Black should forever be grateful. All Donnelly did was retire his first batter in relief 90.5 percent of the time, the best figure by a reliever in all of baseball. He stranded 30 of 34 runners, tops among American League bullpen pitchers. And the league, as a whole, hit a paltry .184 against him.

In the World Series, although it was generally overlooked, he worked seven and one-third scoreless innings. "We couldn't have made it to where we did without him," Scioscia said.

Once Frankie Rodriguez came crashing out of the October clouds, the Angels bullpen, with Donnelly, Rodriguez, and Percival mowing down batter after batter, was almost unbeatable.

So yes, in case you're still wondering, this wasn't just a team with a bunch of emerging stars. It was a role player's delight.

Chapter 8

THE SURREAL POSTSEASON

For so many Angels fans who had waited so long, just the fact that they finally made it to the playoffs seemed reward enough. It had been 16 seasons, going all the way back to that not-so-wonderful year 1986, since their favorite team had the opportunity to play in the postseason.

So the prospect of matching up with the vaunted New York Yankees in the American League Division Series was exciting on its own, especially with the prospect of playing two games back home at Edison Field.

Not even the most ardent of Angels supporters could have imagined what was coming next: the way their team handled Derek Jeter, Bernie Williams, Jason Giambi, and the Yankees in just four pulsating games; the way they then systematically took apart the Central Division champion Minnesota Twins, drowning them in a raging flood of runs, in five games; and that decibel-busting, comeback-raging victory over the San Francisco Giants and superstar Barry Bonds in seven unforgettable World Series games.

The scenario was played out so dramatically and so breath-takingly that it demands a replay. The next few pages will feature a game-by-game account of the Angels' surreal ride through the postseason, followed, in each instance, by new, updated reflections from manager Mike Scioscia. He recounts not only the mood and overall performance of his club, but provides the thinking behind so many of his strategic, and occasionally controversial, moves.

So sit back, relax, and enjoy reliving the greatest October in Angels history.

Chapter 9

THE AMERICAN LEAGUE DIVISION SERIES: WHAT YANKEE MYSTIQUE?

GAME 1

It was the kind of opener most people expected. This is the way they thought the whole series would go. The scrappy Angels would hang in there, push the Yankees hard, but then the team with all the tradition and all the World Series trophies would assert itself and have too much pitching and too much power.

Anaheim ace Jarrod Washburn out-pitched New York starter Roger Clemens. And manager Mike Scioscia's team, thanks to two home runs from third baseman Troy Glaus, actually carried a 5-4 lead into the eighth inning on a typically cool, raucous night in the Bronx.

Then all hell, as well as all that Yankee muscle, broke loose. In a nerve-jangling bottom of the eighth, Scioscia had some tough decisions to make. Reliever Ben Weber recorded two outs and then walked Alfonso Soriano, who takes bases on balls about as often as George Steinbrenner takes the subway. Then Jeter walked. Now Jason Giambi, who already had two hits, including a home run, was coming to the plate. Almost everybody in the park and all Angels fans back home in Orange County expected Scioscia to go with his closer, Troy Percival, in a game of this magnitude.

But he didn't. He went to left-hander Scott Schoeneweis. Giambi hit a rocket, that first baseman Scott Spiezio couldn't handle, into short right field to tie the score. Again, many expected the manager to go to Percival. Again, he went his own way. He went to rookie Brendan Donnelly to pitch to the switch-hitting Bernie Williams. One velvety swing later, Williams homered to break the game open, and the Yankees cruised to an 8-5 victory.

Later, in the postgame interview room, it was obvious how much respect Williams had for the Angels bullpen. "I had not faced Donaldson before," Bernie said, as some reporters quietly chuckled. "Oh, what's the name of that pitcher?" he asked. "Donnelly . . . oh yeah, Donnelly . . ."

Oh yeah, and what Angels critics wanted to know was why Percival and his 98-mph fastball never made it into this game his team needed to win.

SCIOSCIA'S TAKE:

"I know everyone had only one question: Why not Percival? Well, we had Troy figured to get maybe four outs [as opposed to the usual three-out, one-inning appearance] for us sometime during that series. So we had to decide, do we want to stretch Troy to a 30- or 40-pitch inning outing in the very first game, limiting his use in the rest of the games, or should we go with Schoeneweis, who we were very comfortable with in that matchup with Giambi?

"The thing is, we figured if Schoeny walks Giambi, then we could go to Percival. But we were hoping not to bring him in. And once Giambi got that hit, I didn't want to bring Percy into a tie game. That's why we went to Donnelly, who had been throwing the ball great for us. I know it was controversial, but if I had to do it all over again, I'd do it the same way.

"As far as the rest of it was concerned, yeah, it was a tough loss. But I was encouraged overall, because the one thing we wanted to impress on the players, as a staff, is that there is only one way to play baseball. And we were going to play it the same way we had all season. And I think we did that. We played our game. We did some good things early. But as our guys were walking up the tunnel afterwards, you could see they weren't that affected by the loss. They were talking about continuing to play our game and staying positive."

GAME 2

It was almost as if someone gave Mike Scioscia a mulligan in Yankee Stadium. Twenty-four hours after he had opted for someone other than Troy Percival in a clutch, eighth-inning spot, here he was again, facing the same nervous circumstance in the eighth inning of Game 2.

The Angels bats were alive again early, building up a 4-0 lead. But the Yankees came back, narrowing the advantage to 4-3 in the fourth off a shaky Kevin Appier. The sixth was marked by the first appearance of a skinny rookie named Francisco, or Frankie, Rodriguez, whose electric stuff had Scioscia and his coaches enthused after his call-up in mid-September. But this was October, not September, and the kid was treated rudely in his first appearance, although an error by Benji Gil on a potential inning-ending double-play ball didn't help. Pitching to Soriano with the count 0-2, Rodriguez hung a breaking pitch and the power-hitting second baseman crushed it for a three-run homer to give the Yankees a 5-4 lead.

But that's when the Angels gave the first hint of their postseason resiliency. Frankie came back to pitch a solid bridge inning. Then Garret Anderson and Troy Glaus clubbed back-to-back homers off Orlando Hernandez, setting up the eighth-inning scenario everyone had seen the night before. This time there were two outs, not one, and when reliever Weber suffered a weird finger injury, it looked like Percival, who was the only one warming up, would be called in. Only Scioscia again surprised everyone by signaling for Donnelly, who hadn't even been up in the bullpen. The right-hander came in and struck out pinch hitter John Vander Wal. Then, with two outs, it was finally "Percy Time."

Percival came in with two men on and promptly hit Soriano squarely in the left shoulder. So now, on a steamy fall night, the bases were loaded and Derek Jeter, who had gone five for six with two walks so far in the series, was at the plate. Percival never blinked. He worked baseball's most consistent postseason player to a 1-2 count, then struck him out looking with a blur of a fastball on the outside corner. Inning over.

The ninth wasn't any easier. The Yankees scored one run and had two on with the winning run at the plate. Back home in Orange County, you could imagine thousands of Angels fans covering their eyes, afraid to look. They needn't have worried. Percival struck out Nick Johnson, then coaxed Raul Mondesi to pop up to short to end the game and even the best-of-five series at one apiece.

SCIOSCIA'S TAKE:

"The big thing about this game was that we had some key innings to fill in the middle. It was time to see what Francisco could do. Even after he gave up that home run to Soriano, we didn't pull him. We knew we had to be patient. And he wound up throwing great that next inning. That proved to be very important for us the rest of the way.

"Again, in the eighth inning, we didn't want to bring Percy in with one out. If we do, he might have to throw 50 pitches. So we brought in Donnelly, even though he wasn't warming up. I knew Percy was confused, but we weren't. We knew what we wanted to do. It worked out fine for us, even though Percy hit Soriano with his first pitch. He Ks Jeter on a really good fastball on the outside corner and we get out of it.

"It was a big win for us, allowing us to even the series before going home. But we were honestly just trying to play it game by game. That's how we wanted to take it. But looking back, yeah, I think it was really big for our confidence."

GAME 3

Maybe heaven could wait, but Tim Salmon couldn't. Not after he'd already waited longer than anyone in baseball—some 1,388 games—to get to the postseason. Not after he'd endured more of the frustration and futility of this franchise than any of the current players.

So when he finally connected with Steve Karsay's hanging curveball in the eighth inning, sending it soaring into the Edison Field bleachers for the two-run homer that put a lid on a remarkable Angels comeback, the veteran right fielder reacted the same as everyone else. "I had goose bumps," Salmon said, after Scioscia's team had climbed out of a 6-1 sinkhole to beat the Yankees, 9-6, and take a 2-1 lead in the series.

Besides a comeback that featured big hits from Darin Erstad and Salmon, this was a preview of things to come for the Angels. After an emotional Ramon Ortiz struggled early, John Lackey, the rookie who had won nine games in the second half of the season, including the playoff clincher against Texas, worked three important innings of scoreless relief. And then, in the seventh, young Mr. Rodriguez strolled to the mound.

Frankie faced six batters in two innings, striking out four, becoming the first major-league pitcher to get his first two victories in the postseason. "Weren't you scared?" they asked him later. "I'm never afraid; I never fear anything," he said. And he pitched like it.

"The thing I couldn't believe was the crowd noise," said Salmon. "You would have thought we'd won the seventh game of the World Series."

They hadn't—yet.

SCIOSCIA'S TAKE:

"Ramon went out there trying to throw the ball 102 mph. By the third inning, it just didn't look like he was going to get where we needed him to be to stay in the game. He just wasn't showing the patience he displayed in the regular season. We knew Lackey would be valuable in the bullpen for us, and he came in and really gave us a chance to win.

"This was a big game for Frankie. He'd shown some flashes even after he was roughed up a little in Game 2. The way he went after the next four hitters was incredible. So we had a lot of faith in him in Game 3, and he certainly came through. Erstad got the big hit to put us ahead and then Salmon had the big two-run homer. The stadium definitely was alive.

"But this was about more than the atmosphere. What this game showed our club was that we have the ability, in a playoff environment, to come back and score runs against a really good pitching staff. We scored eight unanswered runs after the third inning. You know, when you go into the playoffs for the first time, there is always an unknown element. You don't always know how your team is going to react to the pressure. After this game, we knew. We were reacting just fine."

GAME 4

This was the first of many servings the Angels enjoyed at the Big Inning Buffet. In the bottom half of the fourth, in a tense game that the Yankees led, 2-1, Shawn Wooten, the DH who had fought his way to the big leagues from an independent team in the tiny Saskatchewan town of Moose Jaw, hit a home run. It was as if the Canadian floodgates had opened.

The Angels scored eight runs, pounding out 10 hits during one remarkable 24-pitch span. The rest was left to the bullpen, which was becoming more and more pivotal as the postseason wore on in Anaheim.

Rodriguez once again proved to be the one who stabilized the game, coming in with one out in the seventh. He walked two batters, but he also struck out Jorge Posada and got Johnson to ground out. In the eighth, he was throwing those blurs of his again, striking out two more before giving way to Percival, who gave up three hits but only one run in the ninth to finish up the 9-5 victory and send the Angels to the ALCS.

Wooten had three hits, scored three runs, and drove in two more in the biggest game of his life. In the happy clubhouse afterwards, he talked about his father, who died of lung cancer a year earlier, and how he had talked his son out of quitting baseball when he'd become discouraged after blowing out a knee. "I never would have been where I'm at in life without my dad," Wooten said. "He was my best friend. At his funeral, I let him know he was my best friend. He will always be in my heart."

He will always be on his arm, as well. Wooden wears a large tattoo on his thick left forearm. It reads: "Pops, RIP, 1939-2001."

What happened in Game 4 was no fluke. The Angels hammered the Yankees across four games, batting .376 and collecting 56 hits, an *average* of 14 hits per game. And they beat up on all the best Yankees starters, mugging Roger Clemens, Andy Pettitte, Mike Mussina, and David Wells.

An impressed Derek Jeter said if the Angels continued playing this way, they could win the World Series. Lots of people were starting to agree with him.

SCIOSCIA'S TAKE:

"That inning was amazing. Up until that time, it was the biggest playoff inning I'd ever seen. More important, I liked the way it was happening. It was a lot of situational hitting and going from first to third on base hits. We were in position to win it, so I wanted to go with Washburn [who worked on three days' rest]. He pitched well, but he was running out of gas after five innings. I thought Garret Anderson made a great defensive play early to hold them to one run with that one-handed catch in left field.

"I was proud of our confidence level throughout the whole series. We hung in there and kept going out and playing our style of baseball. I think they were finding out our style was working and they became more comfortable than ever with it. It was big for us; we didn't have to do anything different.

"Our starting pitchers were getting tired, but that was understandable. None of them had ever had to pitch this late in the season before, but, again, that gap was bridged by our middle relief. As soon as we won, I turned my attention toward the next series. I knew Minnesota was a different kind of club from the Yankees. But my main thought was that we had to go out and continue playing our kind of game."

Chapter 10

THE AMERICAN LEAGUE CHAMPIONSHIP SERIES: A TWINS KILLING

GAME I

The Angels had this thing about first games throughout the post-season: they never seemed to get out to a quick start.

On this occasion, in a blaring Metrodome, Minnesota's Joe Mays might as well have spelled his name *Maze*, the way he blocked Mike Scioscia's team at every frustrating twist and turn. This was a pitcher who had been hit hard in Game 2 of the ALDS at Oakland. But it was also the same guy who won 17 games and made the All-Star team a year earlier, before a serious elbow injury sidelined him for much of 2002.

He cut through the heart of Anaheim's lineup like a pitching surgeon, throwing first-ball strikes and keeping the Angels' tough, situational hitters off balance throughout the night. Kevin Appier, who started for the visitors, didn't pitch badly. But he wasn't nearly as sharp as Mays, throwing just 51 strikes in 91 pitches. And eventually, it cost him. He walked Luis Rivas, a weak-hitting No. 9 hitter, and Rivas came in to score the winning run when Corey Koskie lined a double down the right field line in the fifth inning.

This time it was another manager, not Scioscia, who had to make a controversial bullpen decision. Ron Gardenhire pulled Mays, after just 98 pitches, and brought in his closer, Eddie Guardado, in the ninth, even though Guardado had struggled in Game 5 against Oakland. He didn't struggle this time, walking one, but getting the Twins' final three outs and putting the Angels in a 0-1 series hole again.

SCIOSCIA'S TAKE:

"There isn't much to say about this one. Mays pitched great. He never allowed a leadoff hitter on the whole game. He only gave up four hits, and as a result, we could never get into our game. We tried. We tried to work counts, but he had an incredible amount of first strikes, so that made it tough.

"I thought Appier pitched well, and Schoeneweis was fine in relief. But Mays was just too good. We had the same feeling after this one that we had after Game 1 in New York. Our guys knew it was important to get back to our style of baseball in Game 2."

GAME 2

The Angels needed someone to be aggressive, and Brad Fullmer, the DH who is built more like a football player, set the tone.

He ran the bases like a halfback, then muscled up like a fullback, hammering a double and a home run to key a 10-hit attack in a 6-3 victory that evened the series at one. "Yeah, I play baseball with a football player's mentality," said the six-foot, 220-pounder whose picture has appeared in body building magazines. "But a lot of our guys do, I think."

Scott Spiezio scored a big run early when he knocked the ball out of catcher A. J. Pierzynski's glove. David Eckstein and Darin Erstad, the two catalysts at the top of the order, had two hits each and—yes, it is beginning to sound like a recording—the middle relievers, Brendan Donnelly and Frankie Rodriguez, were huge after Scioscia managed to squeeze five less-than-artistic innings out of starter Ramon Ortiz.

But it all started when Fullmer stretched what appeared to be a single in right center into a double in the second inning. That ignited a three-run burst, and the Angels never trailed the rest of the way.

"Today we were a little more aggressive," said Erstad, who had a first-inning homer among his two hits. "This is far and away one of the toughest places I've ever had to play. And we knew we had to win one here." Fullmer agreed. "We're a resilient team. We always bounce back and have fun."

SCIOSCIA'S TAKE:

"The big thing was how aggressive we were early. Spiez stole a run when he knocked the ball out of the catcher's glove. Then we had really good at-bats early. That was a real key. Erstad got us going with a home run. Fullmer came through with some big hits and that hustle double.

"Ortiz bounced back from being too hyper against the Yankees. He didn't have his best stuff, but he gave us a chance to win. We were beginning to realize we could shorten the game, because Frankie was good again and so was Donnelly. It was also the second time in the playoffs that Percy came in and got four outs for us. I think that gave us a lift.

"We knew the Twins' record had been great at home during the playoffs. But we battled them very well at their place. I thought our team looked very comfortable."

GAME 3

This was the Jarrod Washburn the Angels had seen all season and the Troy Glaus they'd been waiting for all year.

Washburn, the smooth left-hander, had won 18 games for the Angels and established himself as the team's clear ace. And on this night, he demonstrated why, pitching seven strong innings, allowing just six hits, with no walks, and striking out seven. The only reason he didn't come away with a victory is that Minnesota's pitchers were almost as sharp.

It was a 1-1 game in the bottom of the eighth when Glaus, with the most natural home-run swing on the team, finally took a pitch the opposite way. All year long, hitting coach Mickey Hatcher had been preaching for him to go to right field more. When Glaus, a right-handed hitter, tried to jerk everything to left, it almost always forced him into a major slump.

This time, though, the advice finally clicked. J. C. Romero tried to paint the outside corner with a fastball and Glaus went with it, sending it into the right field seats to give the Angels a 2-1 victory in a playoff game thick with suspense.

"It was a great piece of hitting, going the other way," said the Twins' Pierzynski, who had the best look at it. "It wasn't a great pitch, but it was a decent pitch. He got enough of it. Shoot, he swings a log. It looks like a 38-ounce bat."

Only the Mets' Mike Piazza has more power to the opposite field, which is why the Angels keep preaching to Glaus to go the other way more. Once he relaxes and does it on a regular basis, there's no telling how many home runs he might hit.

For now, this one was enough to keep Angels fans happy and keep the ThunderStix and the momentum going.

SCIOSCIA'S TAKE:

"This was Washburn's best-pitched game of the postseason. He might have shut them out if [Jacque] Jones hadn't had the big hit to tie it in the seventh. Glaus's home run was good to see. He was making some adjustments at the end of the season, and I think they carried over into the playoffs. It just seemed like he came up with clutch hit after clutch hit.

"Again, we got to use Frankie in the eighth, and if the score had remained tied, we would have gone with him in the ninth. As it was, he struck out two of the three batters he faced. People asked if we were surprised, and we really weren't, at least not by his stuff. We knew he had the pitches to get guys out. But to do it in this kind of setting at age 20, when you realize he was pitching in Double A two months earlier and Triple A a month earlier, well, that was pretty amazing. What he was showing us was that he could be one of the most dominating pitchers in the league."

GAME 4

Call it a baseball purist's kind of game. And the Angels' purest player took it over.

With Minnesota's best pitcher, Brad Radke, and Anaheim's best new starter, rookie John Lackey, dueling, this game was scoreless after seven deliciously tense innings.

That's when Darin Erstad went to work. He singled, stole second, sprinted to third base on a scoring error, and eventually scored the game's first run on Troy Glaus's single. An inning later, another Erstad single kick-started a five-run explosion that put the game away.

"I was fortunate to make contact off him the way [Radke] was throwing," said Erstad. Don't believe him. He would have made contact off Sandy Koufax at that point, he was so determined. Erstad is this team's leader. He sets the tone, on and off the field.

And it was no coincidence that across the full postseason, he was their most consistent player, not only collecting hits by the bucketful, but diving on the ground and crashing into walls to make catches. Erstad plays baseball the way the late Dale Earnhardt used to drive cars.

"I want to enjoy myself in these games," Erstad said. Nobody seemed to be enjoying himself more—unless maybe it was that unflappable rookie again. Frankie Rodriquez worked another inning as a setup man for Troy Percival and racked up two more strikeouts. By now, the raucous crowds at Edison Field were rising en masse and cheering every time he strolled out of the bullpen. You couldn't help but begin to think, is this kid the second coming of Pedro Martinez, or what?

"He is a phenom," said Tim Salmon. "The kid is just amazing."

SCIOSCIA'S TAKE:

"That was a great duel for the first seven innings. After this game, any doubt about whether Lackey was here to stay was wiped away. This kid is going to win a lot of games in the American League.

"He places his fastball well, and then he has a way of dropping that slider under the swing of left-handed hitters. Sometimes, he is more effective against lefties than he is against righties, and that's really unusual. But the best thing about him, the thing that really sells you, is his composure.

"He's going to lose some games like anybody else, but he's not going to lose them because of his composure. There is no question he has the makeup you need to be a championship pitcher."

GAME 5

The sign that appeared a few days later in Edison Field said it all: "Kennedy for President."

Adam Kennedy, the second baseman and No. 9 hitter who quietly led the team in hitting during the regular season, had the kind of breakout game every kid in America dreams about when he is playing wiffleball in the backyard.

Kennedy hit not one, not two, but three home runs—the final one a three-run job after he had fouled off a bunt. It ignited the biggest of all the Angels' postseason innings, a 10-run job, that demolished the Twins, 13-5, and sent this club to its first World Series in forty-two long years.

Only four other players in baseball history have hit three home runs in one playoff game, and one of them was Babe Ruth. But even he didn't have anything on "Babe" Kennedy, who had only seven home runs during the regular season. This was a contact-hitting second baseman whose defense had made a major improvement since the previous season. But he has a long, looping, uppercut of a swing that scouts often cringe at and describe as "unorthodox." It didn't bother him on this unforgettable Sunday, even after Mike Scioscia ordered him to bunt in the seventh inning, although he'd already hit two home runs in the game.

There were two on and nobody out, so Kennedy followed orders. He fouled off one bunt, then Scioscia took off the sacrifice sign. Left-hander Johan Santana got him to swing and foul off another pitch. But the next swing was perfect, and the ball sailed high into the right-center-field bleachers to put the Angels ahead, 6-5, and send the crowd into spasms of delight.

Afterwards, after the Angels had collected a mind-blowing 18 more hits, the Twins were shellshocked. "We ran into a buzz saw," said Minnesota first baseman Doug Mientkiewicz. "Sometimes a team gets three hot guys, and they can carry you for months. But I've never seen nine guys get hot at the same time."

No one was hotter than Kennedy, whose magical line read four for four, with three homers, three runs scored, and five RBIs.

"That's what we're all about," said Scott Spiezio, who had three hits and three RBIs himself. "Getting guys you don't expect to contribute. Like A. K. coming out and hitting three home runs in a game like this. You don't expect that, but he did it."

It was beginning to be a habit for the Angels. They all kept doing things you didn't expect.

SCIOSCIA'S TAKE:

"This one was all about Adam Kennedy. He had an amazing day. I thought Ape [Kevin Appier] gave us some good innings and kept us in it. Donnelly and Rodriguez struggled a little, but again, the key for us is our resilience.

"I think asking Adam to bunt in that spot in the eighth was the right call. Even after he'd hit two home runs. But when he fouled the first bunt attempt off, I noticed the first baseman was really charging in hard, so I took the bunt off. I thought he had a great cut at the next pitch he fouled off. Then he put one great swing on it and hit the three-run homer.

"The big thing for us was not to get too caught up in having another big inning like that. We couldn't let ourselves do that. We didn't want to relax. We wanted to keep going. Making the World Series was incredible. But we didn't want to stop there. We wanted to keep playing our game and win the whole thing."

Chapter 11

THE WORLD SERIES: AND THE FANTASY LIVES

GAME I

Maybe it was just a case of dipping their toes into previously uncharted postseason waters. Maybe it was the enormity of the whole experience suddenly hitting them like a cold October breeze. Maybe it was the intimidating prospect of facing one Barry Bonds. Or maybe it was just the usual first-game blahs that seemed to plague them throughout this nerve-jangling month.

Whatever the reason, for the first time in the postseason, the Angels didn't play like themselves in Game 1 of this wild-card World Series. They were more like the Anti-Angels. They went 0 for 7 with runners in scoring position in the first five innings. They left three runners stranded on third base. They chased high fastballs that sailed out of the strike zone.

And yes, they watched helplessly as Bonds launched a 418-foot home run in his first World Series at-bat off Jarrod Washburn, who clearly seemed to be pitching on fumes in this game. So it was no wonder they lost 4-3 in the opener at Edison Field.

"It just didn't happen tonight," said Darin Erstad, after the Giants utilized three home runs to put Anaheim in its usual 0-1 postseason series hole. "We had our opportunities, but you've got to credit Jason Schmidt. He made pitches when he had to."

Schmidt, the Giants starter, out-pitched Washburn. Bonds and Co. out-homered the Angels 3-2, with Troy Glaus pounding the only two shots for the home team. And most of the bounces seemed to go San Francisco's way. J. T. Snow even made a catch of a Tim Salmon foul popup after falling flat on his back, then scrambling up in time to still grab the baseball. And the Giants bullpen, threatening to be every bit as effective as the Angels, worked three and one-third scoreless and hitless innings.

"It's not like anyone is going to panic," said Anaheim DH Brad Fullmer. "We've been here before."

Shortstop David Eckstein agreed. "We'll keep battling," he said. "This is a long series."

SCIOSCIA'S TAKE:

"Obviously, a lot of our pre-Series strategy revolved around how we intended to pitch Bonds. When he came up leading off the second inning, we decided to challenge him, especially with Wash, the left-hander out there. And you saw what happened. The guy is incredible. We wanted to see what he could do, and he showed us.

"The rest of the game was the way I envisioned the whole Series would go. It was played close, played well defensively, but we just didn't come out on top. You could see Wash was getting a little fuzzy. It had been a long year for him and he was working more innings than he'd ever worked in his career.

"Again, though, I liked the way our guys dealt with the loss. They weren't discouraged. They were still confident. And so was I. I saw a lot of positive things out there in Game 1."

GAME 2

Nobody on the team had waited longer for the Angels' first World Series victory. How appropriate, then, when it finally came, that Tim Salmon would be the hero, collecting four hits and two home runs, including the two-out, two-run shot in the bottom of the eighth that proved the difference in the Angels' surreal 11-10 comeback victory.

Even Disney couldn't have produced it any better. The 34-year-old right fielder, who had been here the longest and suffered the most, came up to deliver the blow that gave the franchise its first Series win.

"It was something I've been dreaming about for a long time and watching it being done from my couch," Salmon said, after hitting the biggest home run of his career. "To go out and do it, to have everything you ever dreamed about doing actually happen, it was just unbelievable."

The game itself was a little hard to believe. It was the second-highest-scoring game in World Series history. And there has been no other Fall Classic, nine-inning match that required the use of 11 pitchers. It was 7-0 Angels, then 9-7 Giants. After seven innings, it was 9-9. And if it seemed like good pitching was at a premium, it was—until Frankie Rodriguez strolled in for another of his remarkable appearances. He entered in the top of the seventh and threw three shutout innings, striking four and utilizing just 26 pitches. It was his work that allowed the Angels to rally with Salmon's two-run homer.

In the ninth, with Troy Percival in to protect a two-run lead, Bonds came up with no one on, and the Angels closer challenged him. The result was the longest home run of this, or maybe any, World Series. The ball seemed to land somewhere on the other side of the 57 freeway. "It was the longest ball I've ever seen hit in this ballpark," said Salmon. Fortunately for the Angels, it only meant one run, and they hung on to win this score-a-thon, 11-10.

SCIOSCIA'S TAKE:

"I thought we started out early playing our kind of game. We knocked [Russ] Ortiz out in the second, and [Brad] Fullmer was able to steal home on the front end of a double steal. That was important. We were back to our style of baseball. But they came back, and before we knew it, we were down in this game.

"Thankfully, our bullpen came in and gave us a big lift. Frankie's three innings were amazing. What did he throw, something like 26 pitches? He gave us a chance to come back. Salmon and our core guys were swinging the bats well, and that always makes things easier for us.

"When Bonds came up in the ninth with a two-run lead and nobody on, we decided to go after him. Well, that ball he hit was the hardest-hit ball I've ever seen. It was incredible. The guy is just an amazing player. But we still had an 11-10 lead, and we had the guy we wanted in Percy out there on the mound. He made his pitches and we finally put it away. It was another big win for us, and it meant we didn't have to go to their place down 0-2."

GAME 3

On a cool, misty night in San Francisco, the Angels reacted with a blizzard of hits. This was, in many ways, their signature performance in the World Series, putting together not one, but two back-to-back innings of batting around. They didn't do it with home runs, either. They did it with lots of singles and doubles and an occasional triple. They racked up sixteen hits overall on the way to a 10-4 mashing of the hometown team in Pac Bell Park.

The big boys like Darin Erstad, Tim Salmon, and Troy Glaus all chipped in, but it was Scott Spiezio, the laid-back first baseman, who led the way. Spiezio lined a game-busting triple and a single to drive in three more runs and creep within three of the postseason RBI record.

"I just try to keep the ball out of the air," Spiezio said. "That's been my philosophy most of the season. If I happen to get one up and it carries out, that's a bonus. But I'm looking to keep it on a line."

The Angels' amazing plate discipline was evident throughout the postseason. David Eckstein, their prime overachiever at shortstop, always talked about "getting to the next pitch," meaning the idea was to foul as many balls off as possible, until you get the pitch you want. If it sounds easy, it isn't. Not against quality major-league pitchers. But the Angels did it to perfection all year, and especially in this game.

Ramon Ortiz, the Anaheim starting pitcher, wasn't great, but he was better than Livan Hernandez, who never made it out of the third inning. And the Angels bullpen, even without the irrepressible Mr. Rodriguez, closed out the four innings in typical shutout style.

SCIOSCIA'S TAKE:

"We got up early in this one, and Ortiz pitched a good game. But then his wrist started to hurt him. He was suffering from a little tendinitis, and we had to look ahead, and start thinking about what we were going to do if this thing went seven games. We knew Lackey was pitching the next game, and we started to think he might be the guy to go to in a possible Game 7.

"Our two four-run innings were great, with us batting around each time. They tried to squeeze back in it with some home runs. But Donnelly and Schoeneweis came in and did a good job. The more of these postseason games we played, the more the overriding theme for us was our bullpen. It was so good and so consistent for us. It gave us a big advantage in every series we played."

GAME 4

The Giants knew something about comebacks, too. They proved it in Game 4, after falling behind 3-0 heading into the bottom of the fifth inning.

Their rally this time was forged not by long, soaring home runs, but by two little infield dribblers. The first, by pitcher Kirk Rueter, turned into a base hit when catcher Bengie Molina elected not to field it. The second, a bunt by Kenny Lofton, rolled on the infield grass, then veered over the foul line heading toward third base. Troy Glaus watched it carefully, reached for it as it went foul, but by the time his hand got there, the ball had wobbled back fair.

On such strange occurrences, World Series often turn. The Giants tied the score in that inning, then pushed across another run, on singles by J. T. Snow and David Bell, in the eighth off the previously untouchable Rodriguez to win this thing, 4-3, and even the Series at two.

"It's good to help the team out," said Snow, the ex-Angel who had a fine Series after a subpar regular season. "But that's the way it goes in baseball. You've got to hang in there and the law of averages eventually comes around."

Snow and closer Robb Nen played high school baseball together at Los Alamitos High in Orange County. Both used to attend Angels games as kids growing up. "I remember watching them play on the same high school team," said Jack Snow, the former NFL Pro Bowl receiver. "Only J. T. was the reliever back then, and he'd come in after Robb. Threw a pretty mean 76-mph fastball on the corners, too."

Nen, who was the Giants' answer to Troy Percival, threw slightly faster than that. And he and the San Francisco bullpen closed this one out with three strong shutout innings.

SCIOSCIA'S TAKE:

"Bell got the big hit off Frankie in this game, and we were eager to see how our guy would come back. He proved he could rebound in the rest of the Series. He showed he could shake it off and that he has a real reliever s mentality.

"Those two infield hits are just baseball. Things like that happen. When Lofton bunted, Glaus was right there. I could see the ball all the way, and it looked like it was going to stay fair, then it looked like it was going foul. At that point, it appeared to hit a pebble or something, and Troy realized then that the ball had shot back fair.

"Like I said, nothing you can do about those things. That's baseball."

GAME 5

In a Series that suddenly felt like a heavyweight slugging match, it was the Giants' turn to explode offensively.

They raked a tired-looking Jarrod Washburn for six runs in the first two innings, allowed the Angels to creep back to within 6-4, then rode the home-run bats of Jeff Kent and Rich Aurilia to a 10-run burst in their final three innings for a 16-4 victory that put them up, 3-2, in the Series.

Bonds continued to cast a huge shadow over this Series, as well. In the second inning, after Lofton singled and Kent doubled, Washburn walked Barry, setting up the second three-run inning of the game. Later, in the sixth, Ben Weber was trying to keep the Angels within two runs, pitching to Kent with Aurilia on first and Bonds in the on-deck circle. Perhaps thinking more about Barry, Weber gave up a two-run homer to Kent, and the game was never close again.

If anything, the lasting snapshot of Game 5 was of J. T. Snow, the first baseman with the soft hands, scooping up three-year-old Darren Baker, the innocent batboy and son of manager Dusty Baker, who looked like he was about to get run over while retrieving a bat at home plate during a Giants rally. Credit J. T. with a save.

And, yes, the momentum seemed to swing back in the Giants' favor as the two teams returned to Anaheim for Game 6. "It's a must win for us," said the Angels' Scott Spiezio, replaying an old refrain. "But it's nothing new for this team. We know how to fight back."

SCIOSCIA'S TAKE:

"It was 6-0 quick, and although we got back to within 6-4, it wasn't enough. They were just swinging the bats incredibly well. They beat us up pretty good.

"I thought the momentum they had built was real. They were getting good pitching and had opened up on offense. When you look back, you realize that from the sixth inning of Game 5 going into the eighth inning of Game 6, they had outscored us, 15-0.

"A lot of teams would quit in that kind of situation. But one thing I knew about our team. We weren't about to give up, momentum or not."

GAME 6

Can you spell classic, boys and girls? This is the game everyone will remember from this World Series. This was the Angels' version of Kirk Gibson and the Dodgers in 1988.

The Giants' Russ Ortiz was pitching the game of his life. The Giants were ahead 5-0 with nine outs to go, and in the visiting clubhouse, the champagne was already on ice. The Angels hitters, so steady all year long, seemed equally cold. They were scoreless in their last nine innings heading into the bottom of the seventh of this one.

Then Troy Glaus singled, followed by a Brad Fullmer single. Manager Dusty Baker had to make a tough decision at that point. Should he stick with Ortiz for another couple of batters, or bring in reliever Felix Rodriguez, who already had worked in all five previous Series games? He brought in Rodriguez to pitch to Scott Spiezio, who worked him hard through a prototypical Angels at-bat.

Eight pitches later, Spiezio lofted an inside fastball high into the air toward right field. It looked like it wouldn't carry far enough, but the breeze, or maybe all those former evil spirits, conspired to take it into the second row of the right-field seats for a three-run homer that closed the gap to 5-3.

"I knew that's all we had to do to get us into one of our hitting frenzies," said bench coach Joe Maddon. The eighth inning began with Erstad, who took a hanging Todd Worrell change-up and ripped it into the right-center-field bleachers. Now it was 5-4, Giants.

Tim Salmon was next up and he singled. Garret Anderson then blooped a single down the left field line. Scioscia had inserted Chone Figgins, Anaheim's swiftest runner, for Salmon at first base. And as he raced toward third on Anderson's hit, Barry Bonds juggled the ball, allowing Anderson to reach second on the error. Baker went to Nenn, his top reliever, but Glaus, who seemed to be getting a big hit every time up, powered a double into the left-center-field alley for a 6-5 lead that sent the red-clad Edison Field crowd into a state of delirium.

When Percival came in and pitched a perfect ninth, the Angels made it official, winning 6-5, recapturing the Series momentum and setting up a seventh-game showdown at Edison the following night.

"I've seen our team pull off some great rallies this year," said shortstop David Eckstein. "But that was amazing."

SCIOSCIA'S TAKE:

"Ortiz was pitching a terrific game for them, and although our guys were facing elimination, they kept battling. Even though they were down 5-0 and had no momentum, our guys still kept a positive attitude in the dugout.

"I knew Spiezio had hit the ball hard, but I thought it was too high. I'm glad I was wrong. I knew that's exactly what we needed.

Now we were in position to do what we do best. Erstad leads off the eighth with a home run, and after Salmon got the hit, it was really important to have Figgins on the bench. He'd been an important weapon for us in the final weeks. And he forced the action on that play. His speed caused Bonds to bobble that ball and get Garret to second. When Glaus hit that double, Garret scored easily. With his bad hamstring, I'm not sure he could have scored from first.

"Looking back, I think that was the best game I've ever been involved in. I was there for the Gibson home-run game with the Dodgers in '88. But after our win in Game 6, our stadium was more electric than any stadium I've ever seen. It was something you know you'll never forget."

GAME 7

They never said it, never talked about it, never fully addressed the issue. But all along, the Angels knew John Lackey was the one they wanted to pitch in Game 7.

They not only liked his stuff, they loved his composure. They knew the rookie right-hander wouldn't get rattled, and he didn't, working five strong innings on only three days' rest, giving up one run and four hits while striking out four.

Although Garret Anderson had been relatively quiet in this Series, Scioscia and everyone else in the home-team dugout knew he was due. And it was his bases-loaded laser of a double down the right-field line that drove in three runs and broke a 1-1 tie in the bottom of the third. That made it 4-1 Angels, and that's how it ended, after two more rookies, Brendan Donnelly and Frankie Rodriguez, got Scioscia's team into the ninth, where an emotional Troy Percival closed out the victory and provided the first World Series title in franchise history.

Edison Field was bedlam afterwards, and Troy Glaus, who was voted the Series MVP, might have summed up the feeling of his celebrating teammates the best. "This is a great honor," he said, holding the MVP trophy. "But we play for the big trophy with the pennants on it, not for these. No one guy on this team has gotten us to this point or carried us through this point. It's been a team effort all the way through—twenty-five guys."

And it was. It was the Series when the best team beat the best player. The whole of the Angels' parts was somehow better than even the eye-popping talent of a player like Barry Bonds.

Jackie Autry celebrates with Disney CEO Michael Eisner after the Angels won the World Series. *AP/WWP*

Edison Field had been cleansed of all the curses and hexes, and Jackie Autry, Gene's widow, could be seen happily waving a lone white Stetson in the cool October sky.

SCIOSCIA'S TAKE:

"John Lackey pitched his heart out for us. He put us in position for Garret to get the big hit. But the big story again was our bullpen. You have to realize that Lackey, Donnelly, and Rodriguez, three rookie pitchers, went eight innings in the seventh game of the World Series to help us win. If I had said that to you in Arizona during spring training, you would have thought I was crazy.

"As I have had a chance to absorb the whole thing, I have come to realize what a tremendous accomplishment it was for our guys. It just validated the respect I had for them all season long.

"I've been in this game a long time, but I've never been around a group of guys so passionate about the game. I couldn't be happier or more proud about what they were able to accomplish."

Chapter 12

MEETING OF THE MINDS

On an unseasonably warm December afternoon in Encino, California, a spry 92-year-old great-grandfather opened the door to his tiny, trophy-filled condominium, smiled, and invited his excited visitor in.

"Thank you, this is a very special treat for me," said Angels manager Mike Scioscia.

"It's my pleasure," said John Wooden. "You know baseball is my favorite sport, don't you?"

"I do know that, and I brought something for you," said Scioscia, handing the legendary former UCLA and Hall of Fame basketball coach a baseball signed by all members of the world champion Angels.

"Oh, thank you, thank you very much," Wooden said.

And so it was that these two men, the great champion of the past and the noted champion of the present, each an admitted fan of the other, sat down for an extended conversation arranged by a reporter. They talked Angels. They talked coaching philosophies. They talked leadership and expectations. But most of all, they talked teamwork, the one common thread that seems to be woven between their winning generations. This, then, is how the discussion went:

WOODEN: "This isn't the first time we've met, you know. Mike escorted me out to the mound when I threw out the first pitch in Game 2 of the World Series. I threw a slider. I threw it about a third of the way and it slid the rest."

SCIOSCIA: "That isn't true. You threw it just fine."

WOODEN: "You know what impressed me the most about your work this year? It's the fact you don't often find teams in any sport without prima donnas. The Angels are one. And that's from you. You did an amazing job, especially after that poor start."

SCIOSCIA: "Thank you, Coach. But I feel lucky to have a team that is basically ego-less. These guys, they all wanted one thing, and that was just to win. I just hope they didn't spoil me."

WOODEN: "What made it so nice is that your team was able to overcome the feats of a player like Barry Bonds. It's amazing to me that more pitchers don't try to force him off the plate. Pitchers I watched through the years, the guys like Gibson and Drysdale and Maglie, they would have had him down."

SCIOSCIA: "We moved him off the plate a little. But you've got to be careful with him. If you try to throw inside, and you miss, you have a problem."

WOODEN: "The way he stands at the plate after he hits a home run offends a lot of people. I remember when basketball players started doing this 360-degree thing in the air before dunking the ball. People asked me what I would have done if a player of mine had done that. I told them I would have had him out of the game before he hit the floor."

SCIOSCIA: "Who was the toughest player you ever had to motivate?"

WOODEN: "One of them was Sidney Wicks. He was the best forward in the country his senior year, but his first year with me he sat on the bench."

SCIOSCIA: "What did you do to get through to him?"

WOODEN: "I used the bench. It was the best ally I had. The key was to get him to be a team player. That's why I was so impressed with what you did. You won without any real All-Stars. You won with a team."

SCIOSCIA: "That's where we were so lucky. Our guys wanted to play like a team. Honestly, it didn't take a lot of convincing. Once we sold our ideas in the spring, preaching situational hitting and moving runners along and keeping players in motion, when somebody didn't execute, the rest of the guys would get on him in the dugout. It was pretty amazing."

WOODEN: "I saw your shortstop [David Eckstein] in the locker room, and I was thinking 'No way. No way.' He looks like he should be on a high school team. But I love the way he plays."

SCIOSCIA: "The thing about Eck is, he's always the smartest guy on the field, and I mean for both teams. What's amazing is that he is really a natural second baseman. He basically learned how to play shortstop at the major-league level, and that's almost unheard of."

WOODEN: "I love the way [Darin] Erstad plays, too. And about that [Frankie] Rodriguez . . . wow!"

SCIOSCIA: "Frankie's incredible. Everyone asks me why we don't try to make him a starter instead of reliever. But we're going to keep him in the bullpen. He's got great makeup. As for Erstad, I played on the same team as Kirk Gibson with the

Dodgers, and I honestly believe Erstad plays on a higher level than Kirk. He is wound tighter than anyone I've ever been around. And this guy does it every pitch of every game, from spring training to the World Series. He practices as hard as he plays more than anybody I've been around."

WOODEN: "What about Garret Anderson? He is very steady, isn't he?"

SCIOSCIA: "I think he's the most misunderstood player on our team. I've said all along, Garret is the best athlete on the team. He has a burning desire to compete, but it just doesn't come to the surface as much because he does everything so easily. If you put a basketball in his hand, I have no doubt he could play that game on a high level. And in football, I bet he would make a great wide receiver."

WOODEN: "What prompted you to change the team's style of play at the start of the season?"

SCIOSCIA: "Our decision wasn't that difficult after our personnel change [the trade of Mo Vaughn]. In 2000, we had four guys who hit 30 home runs. Without all that power, we knew we had to do something different. But the way the guys embraced our idea exceeded all our expectations."

WOODEN: "We did much the same thing with my first NCAA Championship team in 1964. We changed to the press [defense], and it made all the difference that year."

SCIOSCIA: "How did you manage to get so many great players to come to UCLA?"

WOODEN: "This may surprise you, but I never initiated contact with a player outside of California. Never, never. Even with Lewis [Alcindor, aka Kareem Abdul-Jabbar]. A great guard like Mike Warren, he played in high school where I taught in Indiana. His coach played for me, and his assistant was my assistant when I was there at South Bend High. That's how we got him, and Mike proved to be the smartest player I ever had."

SCIOSCIA: "We have the draft. It's a little different from recruiting."

WOODEN: "After our first two national championships, Pauley Pavilion was built and we got Alcindor. That's when we started getting inquiries from players from all over the country. Send us your grades, I'd tell them."

SCIOSCIA: "I have to ask you this, Coach. Who would you take, Alcindor or [Bill] Walton?"

WOODEN: "I'd take either one. But what I've always said is that Alcindor was the most valuable player I've ever had. Walton might have been the best all-around player. Having Alcindor on my team allowed me to understand some things much better. I learned more about man's inhumanity to man by being around him. You wouldn't believe the rude remarks people would say to him, just passing through the airport or in a restaurant."

SCIOSCIA: "Especially after Alcindor, how did you handle the pressure of trying to win year after year?"

WOODEN: "My advice is to let everyone else think and talk about it. Don't you. You can't live in the past. You can only learn from it. Trying to get that across is not always easy. I like to tell the story of this alumnus, who was very influential. We had won nine national championships, including seven in a row at one point, but we had lost in the semifinals against North Carolina State in 1974. Well, the next year, we came back to win the title again in San Diego. And this influential alumnus rushes up to me after the game and says, 'We did it. We did it. You let us down last year, but you made up for it.'"

SCIOSCIA: "You're kidding. The guy really said that? After you'd won nine of 10? That's incredible."

WOODEN: "You know, Mike, what I like about your coaching style is that it is understated. I believe in the more quiet leadership style. I was very fond of [Walter] Alston. I'd spent some time with Gil Hodges and Carl Erskine in Indiana, and they both spoke highly of Alston."

SCIOSCIA: "I was very lucky. I got to meet Alston the first year I came to spring training. He had just retired from managing, and he had taken a job as a consultant with the Dodgers. I guess he kind of took a liking to me, so we spent a lot of time together. He was really an impressive man. It wasn't always so much what he said as it was the way he said it. I felt it was a great privilege to learn from him."

WOODEN: "Did you get a chance to check out some of my baseball souvenirs?"

SCIOSCIA: "I was noticing some of them. I was actually disappointed to see all the Yankees stuff you have here. No, I'm just kidding. Joe Torre is a friend of mine, and someone I have the greatest respect for as a manager."

WOODEN: "I got Derek Jeter's cap right over there."

SCIOSCIA: "That's OK, I see you've also got one of our World Series caps right next to it."

WOODEN: "That's right. And as an Angels fan now, I want you to know we expect it of you regularly now."

SCIOSCIA: "Thanks a lot, Coach. I know you understand. But our fans waited forty-one years for us to finally win a World Series. Now they talk like they expect us to win the next one in forty-one weeks."

WOODEN: "You're right, Mike. I do understand."

Chapter 13

THE ALL-TIME ANGELS

They have been around long enough now. They have won their first world championship. So it is time to decide which of these Angels have been the best. Who belongs on the All-Time Angels team?

Knowing this is certain to spark a rash of debates, it is my privilege as author to take a shot at it. And OK, I admit it. It sounds like fun, too.

So here goes. Having observed and/or covered all these teams through the years, these are my selections as the All-Time Angels:

INFIELDERS

CATCHER: Bob Boone. They called him "Boonie" in the clubhouse, where he exuded a quiet, calm leadership through much of the incendiary 1980s. A magnificent receiver, he was never a great offensive threat. But managers such as Gene Mauch loved him because he could do the little things so well. He could bunt, he could hit and run, he could move runners along. He was Mr. Fundamental.

This has been one of the team's least distinguished positions, so there really wasn't much competition for Boone. Buck Rodgers was a fine catcher who could hit some when he first broke in. But his average and production fell off dramatically after a couple of seasons. Lance Parrish arrived in 1989 and enjoyed a decent year or two, but he was well past his prime.

FIRST BASE: Rod Carew. The smooth-hitting machine who came over from Minnesota didn't play his prime years in Orange County. But he still spewed line drives in every direction, hitting .318, .331, 305, .318, and .339 in one five-year span from 1979–83. He also collected his 3,000th career hit as an Angel in 1985. So, really, what's the big mystery here? When you have a Hall of Famer, you can't go with anyone else unless it is a future Hall of Famer named Albert Pujols. The former Cardinals great signed a $240 million dollar contract in Anaheim, and if he hasn't quite been his old All-World self, he has put up some big power numbers and should put up a few more before he is done.

Some Wally Joyner fans out there might make an argument. The silky left-handed hitter with the good glove enjoyed a couple of spectacular seasons after succeeding Carew at the position, especially 1987, when he hit 34 home runs and drove in 117. The only difference between these two is that Carew did it longer and more consistently than Wally, who eventually leveled off and became a solid .290, 15-homer, 90-RBI type.

Lee Thomas, the man they called "Mad Dog," had a couple of productive years for the expansion Angels, and Scott Spiezio deserves honorable mention for his wonderfully understated two-way performance in 2002.

SECOND BASE: Bobby Grich. Fans who didn't have an opportunity to watch the old Angels, back in the mid-sixties, would think this is a slam-dunk. It really isn't. Bobby Knoop was a wizard with the glove for Bill Rigney's teams, winning Gold Gloves and teaming with Jim Fregosi to form the finest double play combination in franchise history.

But for pure all-around ability, offensively and defensively, you have to give this to Grich. This was the most swashbuckling Angel of them all, a former high school quarterback with home-run power who was a terrific fielder, a fine base runner, and a dashing millionaire who probably made more female hearts flutter than anyone else since Bo Belinsky.

SHORTSTOP: Jim Fregosi. In many ways, he is the quintessential Angel. The team's first franchise player, he was the Derek Jeter of his time—a remarkable athlete who could hit, run, throw, and lead. And he did it all at a remarkably young age.

There is no telling what kind of numbers a young Fregosi might have put up had he played on teams with good hitters surrounding him in the lineup. As it was, he was usually the Angels' only true threat. And yet he still delivered, still played brilliant baseball year after year.

Eventually moving over to become the team manager, Fregosi was always one of Gene Autry's favorites. And no, nobody ever had to ask The Cowboy why.

Gary DiSarcina, the team's rock at the position through much of the frustrating 1990s, would be the runner-up.

THIRD BASE: Troy Glaus. If there was any doubt before the 2002 postseason began, this powerful UCLA alum shattered it with an overwhelming performance in the playoffs and World Series.

He delivered seven home runs overall, topping it off with a three–home run, eight-RBI showcase that made him the Series MVP. After hitting a combined 88 home runs in 2000 and 2001, it was clear that he was going to be a mega-talent. And although he trailed off some during the 2002 regular season, he bounced back to put up those big numbers in October.

The runner-up at the position has to be Doug DeCinces, who came over from the Orioles after replacing Brooks Robinson to have several excellent seasons both offensively and defensively for the Angels in the 1980s. Good-hitting Carney Lansford deserves some honorable mention at the position, too.

OUTFIELDERS

LEFT FIELD: Garret Anderson. When you're the regular-season MVP of the World Series champions and you deliver the key hit in the Game 7 clincher against the Giants, your credentials already are solid. But Anderson's productivity was remarkable even before he dispensed one of the great seasons in franchise history.

A consistent .285-to-.300 hitter, he began developing more power when he hit 35 homers in 2000. He hit 28 in 2001 and had 29 in both 2002 and 2003. More important have been the RBI totals. He drove in 117 in 2000 and 123 each in 2001 and 2002. Often criticized for not diving for balls in the outfield, he was nonetheless a fine defensive player who made difficult catches look easy.

There are several runners-up at this position that we found other spots for on the team. So don't panic.

CENTER FIELD: Mike Trout. This is the easiest pick of the bunch, considering that after only five seasons, Trout is already the finest player in the history of the franchise.

Trout is the Angels' only two-time MVP, and he finished second in that category all three of his other full seasons, a feat never accomplished before in the major leagues.

The numbers are spectacular, but you have to watch him play day in and day out to fully appreciate his extraordinary skills. He is a true five-tool player who hits for average, power, steals bases, and plays a brilliant center field. Some scouts questioned his arm in his first couple of seasons, but he has since worked on that and now throws runners out on a regular basis.

Maybe even more impressive is the joy he exudes playing the game. You'd have to go back to Willie Mays and Pete Rose and maybe throw Ken Griffey Jr. in there, too, to remember a ballplayer that enjoys himself as much. When he isn't on the field, Trout is the first one on the dugout steps to congratulate a teammate on a big hit or a key steal.

In five-plus years, Trout has averaged .306, hit 168 home runs, and added 143 stolen bases. His career OPS is an amazing .963. For the sabermetrics fans out there, Trout has the highest WAR (Wins Above Replacement) number at 48.7 through the age of 24 in baseball history. The only other two players with a WAR above 40 at that stage of their careers are Ty Cobb and Mickey Mantle.

So make room for Trout on the Angels all-time team, and while you're at it, you might also want to start preparing a spot for him in the baseball Hall of Fame.

Honorable mention goes to Albie Pearson, the magnificent leadoff hitter for the club from 1962 to 1966; Fred Lynn, who had all the talent in the world but didn't always utilize it; and Jim Edmonds, who flashed his accomplished all-around skills for an Angels team that brought him up before he was traded to St. Louis in 2000.

RIGHT FIELD: Tim Salmon. Say hello to the most consistent player in the history of the franchise—and easily the best Angels player never to make the All-Star team. From 1993 through 1998, Salmon averaged 29.5 home runs and 97 RBIs per season. Injuries slowed him some, but he bounced back to put up 34 homers and drive in 97 in 2000.

In 2002, he was the feel-good story of the summer, winning the American League Comeback Player of the Year Award and not only producing a quality performance in the playoffs, but wringing every last ounce of enjoyment out of it after waiting 1,388 often frustrating, emotional games to have the experience. In many ways, Tim Salmon is the poster child for everything good and bad that has happened to the Angels.

DESIGNATED HITTERS AND UTILITY PLAYERS

RIGHT-HANDED DH: Vladimir Guerrero. Signed to a five-year, $70 million contract after the 2003 season, Guerrero proved it was money well spent by enjoying six spectacular seasons with the Angels. He won the 2004 American League MVP Award with an eye-popping .337, 39-homer, 126-RBI season. Among the most exciting athletes ever to perform in an Angels uniform, he was a wild free-swinger, yet rarely struck out. He had a powerful arm in right field, even if he did throw more than his share to the wrong base. He hit over .300 in every year but his last with the club, bashed 104 home runs in his first three years in Anaheim, and had 100-plus RBIs four different times. Before he was finished, he set 15 team records. Yes, Big Daddy Vladdy definitely belongs on this all-time team.

LEFT-HANDED DH: Reggie Jackson. Like several of the Angels, Reggie wasn't with the team in the prime of his career. But he was an electric presence, nonetheless, pounding a then-club-record 39 home runs in 1982 and lofting his 500th career home run as a member of this team. Sure, he was more likely to strike out than he was to homer, but it didn't matter. Even when he was taking one of his vicious cuts and missing for strike three, Reggie was exciting to watch. And yes, for those who weren't around, this future Hall of Famer never dogged it. He ran out every ball with everything he had, even with his credentials and accompanying fat wallet. And you had to admire him for that.

UTILITY PLAYER: Darin Erstad. In many ways this is the perfect spot for Erstad, the only player ever to win Gold Gloves at three separate positions—center field, left field, and first base. It should also be noted that Erstad enjoyed the greatest single offensive season in franchise history in 2000, when he batted .355, collected 240 hits, 25 homers, 100 RBIs, and scored 121 runs.

Always at his best in the clutch, Erstad delivered a then-postseason-record 25 hits in 2002, the Angels' World Series winning season.

No one played harder than he did, either. This is a guy who would have thrown his body in front of an Amtrak train if it meant a victory. And his teammates knew it and appreciated it. He not only was one of the Angels' greatest players, he was also one of their greatest leaders.

Honorable mention goes to Brian Downing, the franchise's greatest overachiever, at least until David Eckstein showed up. Downing was a catcher who wound up as a left fielder. He made himself into a professional hitter with good power and an intensity rarely seen in any sport. He and Erstad would have been soul brothers.

PITCHING STAFF

STARTER: Nolan Ryan. Hardly a surprise, is it? The greatest strikeout artist in baseball history wasn't just the best pitcher in the Angels' 56 years, he was the best player—and certainly the biggest gate attraction.

Any time Ryan pitched, you knew you could see a no-hitter. He was an overpowering presence with a fastball that will always rank among the most intimidating pitches in baseball. He struck out 327 or more hitters in five different years and had 156 complete games, winning 138 for the Angels. One of the saddest days this franchise has experienced was when Ryan was allowed to leave and join the Houston Astros as a free agent.

STARTER: Dean Chance. This young, raw-boned Ohio farm boy had the greatest pitching season in Angels history in 1964, winning 20 games, including 11—yes, 11—shutouts and a mind-boggling 1.65 earned-run average.

His buddy, Bo Belinsky, got more headlines early in their careers, but Chance was a far better pitcher and might have been a Hall of Fame candidate if he had taken better care of himself off the field.

STARTER: Chuck Finley. The team's all-time victory leader with 140, 19 more than Ryan, the tall blond left-hander never had one overwhelming season, but was the "horse" of this staff through much of the raucous 1990s. He was always there, through good times and bad, even rushing in as the first one to help save his manager Buck Rodgers's life in the terrible team bus accident of 1992.

He still ranks as the career leader in starts (379) and innings pitched (2,675) in addition to victories.

STARTER: Frank Tanana. He was the other half of the two-man rotation that some called "Tanana and Ryan, and Then Start Cryin." A tall, fastball-conscious lefty with terrific stuff, he still ranks just beyond Ryan in team shutouts with 24 and is fifth on the all-time strikeout list with 1,233.

An arm injury changed him from a power pitcher to a guy who had to get by on finesse and guile, which he managed to do with several teams after leaving the Angels.

STARTER: Tie between Jim Abbott and Jared Weaver. Yeah, OK, so Abbott is something of a sentimental pick. So what? You shouldn't have to apologize for naming the most courageous player in Angels history to this team. A young man born without a right hand, Abbott nonetheless made it to the big leagues and became an inspiration to millions throughout the world.

Besides, he won 40 games from 1989 to 1991, including an 18-victory, 2.89-ERA season in '91. And his first major-league shutout, when he outpitched Boston's Roger Clemens in Anaheim, remains one of the more magical nights the franchise has produced.

Weaver is the second-winningest pitcher in Angels history behind Chuck Finley with 150 victories. The former Long Beach State All-American, with a body that resembled your basic Southern California surfboard, dispensed some of the most memorable seasons in Angels history, going 20–5 with a 2.81 ERA in 2012, 18–8 and 2.41 in 2011, and 18–9 in 2014.

He had a long run as Mike Scioscia's ace before his fastball started to lose its velocity. But even without his best stuff the past couple of years, Weaver was a fierce competitor who finessed his way to his share of victories. A free agent at the end of 2016, he left to join the San Diego Padres.

Mike Witt, the Angels' third-winningest pitcher, deserves honorable mention, along with Mark Langston, Ken McBride, Andy Messersmith, Clyde Wright, and George Brunet.

CLOSER: Troy Percival. Another slam-dunk selection, especially after the way he and his 96-mph fastball rattled their way through that memorable October in 2002. Percy is the Angels' all-time career record holder in saves with 316.

This has been one of the more productive positions in club history, though, and among those who deserve honorable mention are Bryan Harvey, Minnie Rojas, Bob Lee, and, yes, the late Donnie Moore.

MANAGER

MANAGER: Bill Rigney. He pumped life into the organization early, not only shaping the club in its first year, but taking a scruffy, second-year expansion team to what was the most remarkable season in the history of the franchise, until 2002, of course.

"Rig" was a players' manager who was years ahead of his time in making moves and strategizing. And no one was ever more popular with the writers. Managing eight-plus years with teams never infused with overwhelming talent, he still managed to win 80 or more games four different times.

Gene Mauch will be remembered most for his two painful near misses in 1982 and 1986, but he deserves better than that. No one knew as much about baseball as this man, who won 90-plus games three different times with the Angels, a feat no one else has accomplished. Jim Fregosi deserves mention for managing the team to its first division title in 1979. And Mike Scioscia, easily the longest-tenured manager in franchise history, could eventually move up to the No. 1 spot, especially if he can somehow maneuver the Angels back into World Series contention. But for now, the extraordinary magic Rigney created in the early years of his reign is simply too much to overcome.